GW00818918

cooking with **pasta**

cooking with **pasta**

Over 50 fresh & innovative
Italian recipes

JENI WRIGHT

HERMES
HOUSE

For all recipes, **quantities** are given in both **metric** & **imperial** measures &, where appropriate, measures are also given in **standard cups** & **spoons**. Follow one set, but not a mixture, because they are **not interchangeable**.

Standard **spoon** & **cup measures** are level.
1 tsp = 5 ml, 1 tbsp = 15 ml, 1 cup = 250 ml/8 fl oz

Australian standard **tablespoons** are 20 ml. Australian readers should use 3 tsp in place of 1 tbsp for measuring small quantities of gelatine, cornflour, salt, etc.

Medium eggs are used unless otherwise stated.

The recipes in this book have been extracted from a larger book The Pasta Bible.

First published in 1999 by Hermes House

© Anness Publishing Limited 1999

Hermes House is an imprint of Anness Publishing Limited
Hermes House, 88–89 Blackfriars Road, London SE1 8HA.

All rights reserved. No part of this publication may be reproduced, stored in a retrieval system or transmitted in any way or by any means, electronic, mechanical, photocopying, recording or otherwise, without the prior written permission of the copyright holder.

ISBN 1 84038 499 9

A CIP catalogue record for this book is available from the British Library

Publisher Joanna Lorenz
Executive cookery editor Linda Fraser
Senior editor Doreen Palamartschuk
Copy editors Linda Doeser & Jenni Fleetwood
Design Wherefore Art?
Photography William Lingwood & Janine Hosegood
Food for photography Lucy McKelvie & Kate Jay
Styling Clare Louise Hunt

Printed & bound in Singapore
10 9 8 7 6 5 4 3 2 1

cooking WITH pasta

introduction

Pasta is one of the **most popular** foods in the world today. Available in an **amazing** range of shapes and flavours, it is incredibly versatile, and can be served in scores of different ways. **People love it** for the **energy** it gives them at low cost, chefs delight in introducing light and healthy sauces for modern palates and families often **favour bakes** that can be cooked ahead and which will stretch to **serve** extra guests. **Simple** or sophisticated, quick and easy to cook, it is the perfect choice for **everyday** and spur-of-the-moment meals.

pasta shapes

THE MANY HUNDREDS OF **DIFFERENT TYPES** OF **FRESH** AND **DRIED** PASTA ARE DIVIDED INTO CATEGORIES. **LONG**, **SHORT** AND **FLAT** SHAPES ARE THE MOST COMMON, BUT THERE ARE ALSO **STUFFED** SHAPES, SHAPES **SUITABLE** FOR STUFFING AND **TINY** SHAPES FOR **USE IN SOUP**. AMONG THESE, YOU WILL FIND SOME LESS WELL-KNOWN **REGIONAL** SHAPES AND THE **MORE UNUSUAL** AND **DECORATIVE DESIGNER** SHAPES.

ONLY BUY **DRIED PASTA** THAT IS MADE USING **100% DURUM WHEAT**. IF YOU DECANT PASTA SHAPES INTO STORAGE JARS, USE UP ANY **REMAINING PASTA** BEFORE ADDING MORE FROM A **NEW PACKET**. OLDER PASTA MAY TAKE **LONGER TO COOK** THAN THAT FROM A **FRESHER PACKET**, AND SOME **BRANDS MAY NOT** NECESSARILY HAVE THE **SAME COOKING TIME**. FRESH PASTA WILL COOK VERY QUICKLY.

LONG PASTA

Dried long pasta (pasta lunga) in the form of spaghetti is probably the best-known pasta of all time, and was certainly one of the first types to be exported from Italy. Spaghetti is still very widely used, but nowadays there are many other varieties of fresh and dried long pasta that look and taste even better. Long pasta comes in different lengths, but 30cm/12in is about the average. Many long shapes are available in plain durum wheat only.

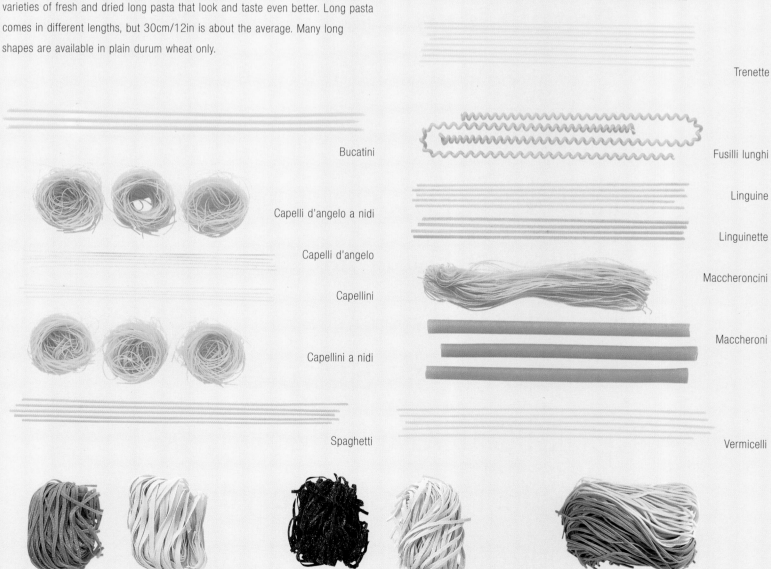

Bucatini

Capelli d'angelo a nidi

Capelli d'angelo

Capellini

Capellini a nidi

Spaghetti

Pappardelle

Trenette

Fusilli lunghi

Linguine

Linguinette

Maccheroncini

Maccheroni

Vermicelli

Fresh tagliatelle verdi and tagliatelle all'ouvo

Fresh taglialini with squid ink and taglialini all'ouvo

Fresh paglia e fieno

SHORT PASTA

There are literally hundreds of different short pasta (pasta corta) shapes, and new ones are constantly coming into our shops. Some people prefer short pasta simply because it is easier to cook and eat than long pasta. It also goes well with many different sauces, and in most cases you can literally choose any shape you fancy, regardless of whether your sauce is a smooth tomato, cream or olive oil based type, or is chunky with large pieces of fish, meat or vegetables.

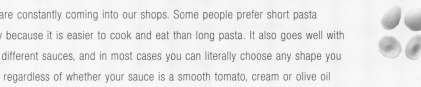

Orecchiette

Rigatoni

Strozzapreti

Tubetti

Conchiglie rigate

Eliche all'ouvo

Fusilli con spinace

Maccheroni

Maccheroncelli

Farfalle

Conchiglioni rigate

Stortini

Fusilli

Penne rigate

Rotelle tricolore

STUFFED PASTA

The most common dried stuffed pasta shapes are tortellini (little pies), a speciality of Bologna. They are made from rounds or circles of pasta, so they look like little plump rings, another name for which is anolini. Some Italian delicatessens also sell dried cappelletti (little hats), which resemble tortellini but are made from squares of pasta and so have little peaks. Cappelletti are a speciality of Emilia-Romagna, and are more likely to be sold fresh than dried. The same goes for ravioli.

Fresh ravioli all'uovo

Fresh agnolotti all'uovo

Tortellini verdi

FLAT PASTA

Although there are many kinds of long flat ribbon pasta such as fettuccine and tagliatelle, there is really only one broad, flat pasta used for baking in the oven (al forno), and that is lasagne. Thin sheets of lasagne are designed to be baked between layers of sauce in the oven, or cooked in boiling water until al dente, rolled around a filling to make cannelloni, then baked in the oven. All types of lasagne are designed to be used in this way, and are never served with a separate sauce.

Crimped lasagne verdi

Plain lasagnette, crimped on one side

PASTA FOR STUFFING

Large pasta shapes (pasta da ripieno) are made commercially for stuffing and baking in the oven. Fillings vary enormously, from meat and poultry to spinach, mushrooms and cheese, and the pasta can be baked in either a creamy béchamel or a tomato sauce. They do not need to be boiled before being stuffed.

Cannelloni

DRIED PASTA FOR SOUP

Teeny-weeny pasta shapes are called pastina in Italian, and there are literally hundreds of different ones to choose from. They are mostly made from plain durum wheat, although you may find them with egg and even flavoured with carrot or spinach. In Italy they are always served in broths and clear soups and vary in size and shape.

Alfabeto

Stellini

soups & broths

rich minestrone

THIS IS A **SPECIAL** MINESTRONE MADE WITH CHICKEN. **SERVED** WITH **CRUSTY** ITALIAN BREAD, IT MAKES A **HEARTY** MEAL.

method

SERVES 4–6

1 Heat the oil in a large frying pan. Add the chicken thighs and fry for about 5 minutes on each side. Remove from the pan with a slotted spoon and set aside.

2 Lower the heat, add the bacon, onion and herbs to the pan and stir well. Cook gently, stirring constantly for about 5 minutes. Add all the vegetables, except the frozen peas and cook, stirring frequently, for 5–7 minutes more.

3 Return the chicken thighs to the pan, add the stock and bring to the boil. Cover and cook over a low heat, stirring occasionally, for about 35–40 minutes.

4 Remove the chicken thighs with a slotted spoon and place them on a board. Stir the peas and pasta into the soup and bring back to the boil. Simmer, stirring frequently, for 7–8 minutes, until the pasta is tender, but still firm to the bite.

5 Meanwhile, remove and discard the chicken skin, then remove the meat from the bones and cut it into 1cm/½in pieces. Return the meat to the soup and heat through. Taste for seasoning. Ladle the soup into individual soup bowls, scatter over the Parmesan shavings and garnish with one or two basil leaves. Serve immediately.

---

cook's tip
For extra flavour, add any Parmesan rind to the simmering soup.

---

ingredients

15ml/1 tbsp extra virgin
olive oil
2 **chicken** thighs
3 rindless **streaky bacon**
rashers, chopped
1 **onion**, finely chopped
a few fresh **basil**
leaves, shredded
a few fresh **rosemary leaves**,
finely chopped
15ml/1 tbsp chopped fresh **flat**
leaf parsley
2 **potatoes**, cut into
1cm/½in cubes
1 large **carrot**, cut into
1cm/½in cubes
2 small **courgettes**, cut into
1cm/½in cubes
1–2 **celery** sticks, cut into
1cm/½in cubes
1 litre/1¾ pints/4 cups
chicken stock
200g/7oz/1¾ cups **frozen peas**
90g/3½oz/scant 1 cup dried
stellette or other soup pasta
salt and freshly ground
black pepper
coarsely shaved **Parmesan**
cheese and fresh **basil**
leaves, to garnish

ingredients

1 **onion**

2 **celery** sticks

1 large **carrot**

45ml/3 tbsp **olive oil**

150g/5oz **French beans**, cut
   into 5cm/2in pieces

1 **courgette**, thinly sliced

1 **potato**, cut into 1cm/½in cubes

¼ **Savoy cabbage**, shredded

1 small **aubergine**, cut into
   1cm/½in cubes

200g/7oz can **cannellini
   beans**, drained and rinsed

2 Italian **plum
   tomatoes**, chopped

1.2 litres/2 pints/5 cups
   vegetable stock

90g/3½oz dried **spaghetti**
   or **vermicelli**

salt and freshly ground
   black pepper

For the pesto

about 20 fresh **basil leaves**

1 **garlic** clove

10ml/2 tsp **pine nuts**

15ml/1 tbsp freshly grated
   Parmesan cheese

15ml/1 tbsp freshly grated
   Pecorino cheese

30ml/2 tbsp **olive oil**

genoese minestrone

IN **GENOA** THEY OFTEN MAKE **MINESTRONE** LIKE THIS, WITH **FRESH PESTO** STIRRED IN AT THE END OF COOKING. IT IS AN **EXCELLENT** SUPPER DISH.

method

SERVES 4–6

1 Finely chop the onion, celery and carrot, either in a food processor or by hand. Heat the oil in a large saucepan, add the chopped mixture and cook over a low heat, stirring frequently, for 5–7 minutes.

2 Mix in the French beans, courgette, potato and cabbage. Stir-fry over a medium heat for about 3 minutes. Add the aubergine, cannellini beans and tomatoes and stir-fry for 2–3 minutes more. Pour in the stock with salt and pepper to taste. Bring to the boil. Stir well, cover and lower the heat. Simmer for 40 minutes, stirring occasionally.

3 Meanwhile, process all the pesto ingredients in a food processor until the mixture forms a smooth sauce, adding 15–45ml/1–3 tbsp water through the feeder tube, if necessary.

4 Break the pasta into small pieces and add it to the soup. Simmer, stirring frequently, for 5 minutes. Stir in the pesto sauce, then simmer for 2–3 minutes more, or until the pasta is tender, but still firm to the bite. Taste for seasoning. Serve hot, in warmed soup plates or bowls.

roasted tomato & pasta soup

WHEN THE ONLY **TOMATOES** YOU CAN BUY ARE **NOT** PARTICULARLY **FLAVOURSOME**, MAKE THIS SOUP. THE **ROASTING COMPENSATES** FOR ANY **LACK** OF **FLAVOUR** IN THE TOMATOES, AND THE SOUP HAS A WONDERFUL **SMOKY TASTE**.

method

SERVES 4

1 Preheat the oven to 190°C/375°F/Gas 5. Spread out the tomatoes, red pepper, onion and garlic in a roasting tin and drizzle with the olive oil. Roast for 30–40 minutes, until the vegetables are soft and charred, stirring and turning them after 15–20 minutes.

2 Tip the vegetables into a food processor, add about 250ml/8fl oz/ 1 cup of the stock or water and process until puréed. Scrape into a sieve placed over a large saucepan and press the purée through with the back of a wooden spoon into the pan.

3 Add the remaining stock or water, the sugar and salt and pepper to taste. Bring to the boil, stirring.

4 Add the pasta and simmer, stirring frequently, for 7–8 minutes, or until tender but still firm to the bite. Taste for seasoning. Serve hot in warmed bowls, garnished with the fresh basil.

cook's tips
To save time, you can roast the vegetables in advance. Allow them to cool, then leave them in a covered bowl in the fridge overnight before puréeing. The soup can be frozen without the pasta. Thaw and bring to the boil before adding the pasta.

ingredients

450g/1lb ripe Italian **plum tomatoes**, halved lengthways
1 large **red pepper**, quartered lengthways and seeded
1 large **red onion**, quartered lengthways
2 **garlic** cloves, unpeeled
15ml/1 tbsp **olive oil**
1.2 litres/2 pints/5 cups **vegetable stock** or **water**
good pinch of **sugar**
90g/3½oz/scant 1 cup dried small **pasta shapes**, such as **tubetti** or small **macaroni**
salt and freshly ground **black pepper**
fresh **basil leaves**, to garnish

THIS IS A **CALABRIAN** SPECIALITY. ITS **ITALIAN** NAME COMES FROM THE WORD **MILLECOSE**, MEANING "**A THOUSAND THINGS**". LITERALLY **ANYTHING** EDIBLE CAN GO INTO THIS **SOUP**. IN CALABRIA THEY INCLUDE A **BEAN** CALLED **CICERCHIA** THAT IS PECULIAR TO THIS SOUTHERN REGION.

pasta, bean & vegetable broth

ingredients

75g/3oz/scant ½ cup **brown lentils**
475ml/16fl oz/2 cups **water**
15g/½oz dried **mushrooms**
175ml/6fl oz/¾ cup **hot water**
60ml/4 tbsp **olive oil**
1 **carrot**, diced
1 **celery stick**, diced
1 **onion**, finely chopped
1 **garlic** clove, finely chopped
15ml/1 tbsp chopped fresh **flat leaf parsley**
a pinch of crushed dried **red chillies** (optional)

1.5 litres/2½ pints/6¼ cups **vegetable stock**
150g/5oz/scant 1 cup each canned **red kidney beans**, **cannellini beans** and **chick-peas**, rinsed and drained
115g/4oz/1 cup dried small **pasta shapes**, such as **rigatoni**, **penne** or **penne rigate**
salt and freshly ground **black pepper**
chopped **flat leaf parsley**, to garnish
Pecorino cheese, to serve

method

SERVES 4–6

1 Put the lentils in a medium saucepan, add the cold water and bring to the boil over a high heat. Lower the heat to a gentle simmer and cook, stirring occasionally, for 15–20 minutes, or until the lentils are just tender. Meanwhile, put the dried mushrooms in a small bowl with the hot water. Set aside to soak for 15–20 minutes.

2 Tip the lentils into a sieve to drain, then rinse under cold running water. Drain the soaked mushrooms and reserve the soaking liquid. Finely chop the mushrooms and set aside.

3 Heat the oil in a large saucepan and add the carrot, celery, onion, garlic, parsley and chillies, if using. Cook over a low heat, stirring constantly, for 5–7 minutes.

4 Add the stock, then the mushrooms and their soaking liquid. Bring to the boil, then add the beans, chick-peas and lentils, with salt and pepper to taste. Cover, and simmer gently for 20 minutes.

5 Add the pasta and bring the soup back to the boil, stirring. Simmer, stirring frequently, for 7–8 minutes, until the pasta is tender but still firm to the bite. Season, then serve hot in soup bowls, garnished with parsley with grated Pecorino cheese served separately.

ingredients

1 **onion**

2 **carrots**

2 **celery** sticks

60ml/4 tbsp **olive oil**

400g/14oz can **chick-peas**,
    rinsed and drained

200g/7oz can **cannellini**
    beans, rinsed and drained

150ml/¼ pint/⅔ cup **passata**

120ml/4fl oz/½ cup **water**

1.5 litres/2½ pints/6¼ cups
    vegetable or **chicken stock**

2 fresh or dried
    rosemary sprigs

200g/7oz/scant 2 cups dried
    conchiglie

salt and freshly ground
    black pepper

freshly grated **Parmesan**
    cheese, to serve

variations

You can use other pasta shapes, but
conchiglie are ideal because they
scoop up the chick-peas and beans.
If you like, crush 1–2 garlic cloves
and fry them with the vegetables.

pasta &
chick-pea soup

A **SIMPLE**, COUNTRY-STYLE SOUP. THE
SHAPE OF THE **PASTA** AND THE **BEANS**
COMPLEMENT ONE ANOTHER **BEAUTIFULLY**.

method

SERVES 4–6

1 Finely chop the onion, carrots and celery, either in a food processor
or with a sharp knife.

2 Heat the oil in a large saucepan, add the chopped vegetable mixture
and cook over a low heat, stirring frequently, for 5–7 minutes.

3 Add the chick-peas and cannellini beans, stir well to mix, then cook
for 5 minutes. Stir in the passata and water. Cook, stirring, for
2–3 minutes.

4 Add 475ml/16fl oz/2 cups of the stock, one of the rosemary sprigs
and salt and pepper to taste. Bring to the boil, cover, then simmer
gently, stirring occasionally, for 1 hour.

5 Pour in the remaining stock, add the pasta and bring to the boil,
stirring. Lower the heat and simmer, stirring frequently, for about
7–8 minutes, or until the pasta is tender but still firm to the bite. Taste
for seasoning. Remove the rosemary sprig and serve the soup hot, in
warmed individual bowls, topped with grated Parmesan and a few
rosemary leaves.

farmhouse broth

ROOT VEGETABLES FORM THE BASE OF THIS **CHUNKY**, MINESTRONE-STYLE **MAIN MEAL** SOUP. YOU CAN **VARY** THE **VEGETABLES** ACCORDING TO WHAT YOU HAVE TO HAND.

method

SERVES 4

1 Heat the oil in a large saucepan, add the onion and cook over a low heat for about 5 minutes, until softened. Add the fresh vegetables, canned tomatoes, tomato purée, dried herbs and dried peppers, if using. Stir in salt and pepper to taste.

2 Pour in the stock or water and bring to the boil. Stir well, cover, lower the heat and simmer for 30 minutes, stirring occasionally.

3 Add the pasta and bring to the boil, stirring. Lower the heat and simmer, uncovered, stirring frequently, for about 5 minutes, or until the pasta is tender but still firm to the bite.

4 Stir in the beans. Heat through for 2–3 minutes, then remove from the heat and stir in the parsley. Taste the soup for seasoning. Serve hot in warmed soup bowls, with grated Parmesan served separately.

---

cook's tip

Packets of dried Italian peppers are sold in many supermarkets and in delicatessens. They are piquant and firm with a "meaty" bite to them, which makes them ideal for adding substance to vegetarian soups.

---

ingredients

30ml/2 tbsp **olive oil**

1 **onion**, roughly chopped

3 **carrots**, cut into large chunks

175–200g/6–7oz **turnips**, cut into large chunks

about 175g/6oz **swede**, cut into large chunks

400g/14oz can chopped **plum tomatoes**

15ml/1 tbsp **tomato purée**

5ml/1 tsp dried **mixed herbs**

5ml/1 tsp dried **oregano**

50g/2oz/½ cup dried **peppers**, washed and thinly sliced (optional)

1.5 litres/2½ pints/6¼ cups **vegetable stock** or **water**

50g/2oz/½ cup dried **elbow macaroni** or **conchiglie**

400g/14oz can **red kidney beans**, rinsed and drained

30ml/2 tbsp chopped fresh **flat leaf parsley**

salt and freshly ground **black pepper**

freshly grated **Parmesan cheese**, to serve.

clam & pasta soup

SUBTLY SWEET AND **SPICY**, THIS SOUP IS **SUBSTANTIAL** ENOUGH TO BE SERVED ON ITS OWN FOR **LUNCH** OR **SUPPER**. A **CRUSTY** ITALIAN **LOAF,** SUCH AS **PUGLIESE** OR **CIABATTA** IS THE **PERFECT** ACCOMPANIMENT.

ingredients

30ml/2 tbsp **olive oil**

1 **onion**, finely chopped

leaves from 1 fresh or dried
  thyme sprig, chopped, plus
  extra to garnish

2 **garlic** cloves, crushed

5–6 fresh **basil leaves**, plus
  extra to garnish

1.5–2.5ml/¼–½ tsp crushed
  dried **red chillies**, to taste

1 litre/1¾ pints/4 cups
  fish stock

350ml/12fl oz/1½ cups **passata**

5ml/1 tsp **sugar**

90g/3½oz/scant 1 cup
  frozen peas

65g/2½oz/⅔ cup dried
  small **pasta shapes**, such
  as **chifferini**

225g/8oz frozen shelled **clams**
  or bottled clams in their shells

salt and freshly ground
  black pepper

method

SERVES 4–6

1 Heat the oil in a large saucepan, add the onion and cook gently for about 5 minutes, until softened, but not coloured. Add the thyme, then stir in the garlic, basil leaves and chillies.

2 Add the stock, passata and sugar to the saucepan, with salt and pepper to taste. Bring to the boil, then lower the heat and simmer gently, stirring occasionally, for 15 minutes. Add the frozen peas and cook for a further 5 minutes.

3 Add the pasta to the stock mixture and bring to the boil, stirring. Lower the heat and simmer, stirring frequently, for about 5 minutes, or until the pasta is tender but still firm to the bite.

4 Turn the heat down low, add the frozen or bottled clams and heat through for 2–3 minutes. Taste for seasoning. Serve hot in warmed bowls, garnished with basil and thyme.

cook's tip
Frozen shelled clams are available at good fishmongers and supermarkets; if you can't get them, use bottled or canned clams in natural juice (not vinegar). Italian delicatessens sell jars of clams in their shells. These both look and taste delicious and are not too expensive. For a special occasion, stir some into the soup.

meatball & pasta soup

EVEN THOUGH THIS **SOUP** COMES FROM **SUNNY SICILY**, IT IS **SUBSTANTIAL** ENOUGH FOR A **HEARTY SUPPER** ON A **WINTER'S DAY**.

method

SERVES 4

1 Make the meatballs. Break the bread into a small bowl, add the milk and set aside to soak. Meanwhile, put the minced beef, garlic, Parmesan, parsley and egg in another large bowl. Grate fresh nutmeg liberally over the top and add salt and pepper to taste.

ingredients

2 x 300g/11oz cans **condensed beef consommé**
90g/3½oz/¾ cup dried very **thin pasta**, such as **fidelini** or **spaghettini**
fresh **flat leaf parsley**, to garnish
freshly grated **Parmesan cheese**, to serve

For the meatballs
1 very thick slice of **white bread**, crusts removed
30ml/2 tbsp **milk**
225g/8oz/1 cup **minced beef**
1 **garlic** clove, crushed
30ml/2 tbsp freshly grated **Parmesan cheese**
30–45ml/2–3 tbsp chopped fresh **flat leaf parsley**
1 **egg**
nutmeg
salt and freshly ground **black pepper**

2 Squeeze the bread with your hands to remove as much milk as possible, then add the bread to the meatball mixture and mix everything together well with your hands. Wash your hands, rinse them in cold water, then form the mixture into tiny balls about the size of small marbles.

3 Tip both cans of consommé into a large saucepan, add water as directed on the labels, then add an extra can of water. Stir in salt and pepper to taste and bring to the boil.

4 Drop in the meatballs, then break the pasta into small pieces and add it to the soup. Bring the soup to the boil, stirring gently. Simmer, stirring frequently, for 7–8 minutes, or until the pasta is tender but still firm to the bite. Taste for seasoning. Serve hot in warmed bowls, sprinkled with chopped parsley, with freshly grated Parmesan cheese served separately.

ingredients

115g/4oz/⅔ cup **chicken livers**,
   thawed if frozen
3 sprigs each fresh **parsley**,
   marjoram and **sage**
leaves from 1 fresh
   thyme sprig
5–6 fresh **basil leaves**
15ml/1 tbsp **olive oil**
knob of **butter**
4 **garlic** cloves, crushed
15–30ml/1–2 tbsp **dry**
   white wine
2 x 300g/11oz cans **condensed**
   chicken consommé
225g/8oz/2 cups **frozen peas**
50g/2oz/½ cup dried **pasta**
   shapes, such as **farfalle**
2–3 **spring onions**,
   sliced diagonally
salt and freshly ground
   black pepper

pasta soup with chicken livers

A SOUP THAT CAN BE SERVED AS **EITHER** A **FIRST** OR **MAIN COURSE**. THE FRIED **FEGATINI** ARE SO **DELICIOUS** THAT EVEN IF YOU DO NOT **NORMALLY** LIKE **CHICKEN LIVERS** YOU WILL FIND YOURSELF **LOVING** THEM IN THIS SOUP.

method

SERVES 4–6

1 Cut the chicken livers into small pieces with scissors. Chop the herbs. Heat the oil and butter in a frying pan, add the garlic and herbs, with salt and pepper to taste, and fry gently for a few minutes. Add the livers, increase the heat to high and stir-fry for a few minutes, until they change colour and become dry. Pour the wine over the livers, cook until the wine evaporates, then remove the livers from the heat and taste for seasoning.

2 Tip both cans of condensed chicken consommé into a large saucepan and add water to the condensed soup as directed on the labels. Add an extra can of water, then stir in a little salt and pepper to taste and bring to the boil.

3 Add the frozen peas to the pan and simmer for about 5 minutes, then add the small pasta shapes and bring the soup back to the boil, stirring constantly. Lower the heat and simmer, stirring frequently, for about 5 minutes, or until the pasta is tender but still firm to the bite.

4 Add the fried chicken livers and spring onions and heat through for 2–3 minutes. Taste for seasoning. Serve hot, in warmed bowls.

cream sauces

pipe rigate with peas & ham

PRETTILY FLECKED WITH **PINK** AND **GREEN**, THIS IS A **LOVELY DISH** FOR A **SPRING** OR **SUMMER** SUPPER **PARTY**.

method

SERVES 4

1 Melt half the butter with the olive oil in a medium saucepan until foaming. Add the thawed frozen peas and the crushed garlic to the pan, followed by the chicken stock, wine or water.

2 Sprinkle in the chopped parsley and add salt and pepper to taste. Cook over a medium heat, stirring frequently, for 5–8 minutes, or until most of the liquid has been absorbed.

3 Add about half the cream, increase the heat to high and let the cream bubble, stirring constantly, until it thickens and coats the peas. Remove from the heat, stir in the ham and taste for seasoning.

4 Cook the pasta in a large saucepan of lightly salted boiling water for 8–10 minutes until tender but still firm to the bite. Tip into a colander and drain well.

5 Immediately melt the remaining butter with the cream in the pan in which the pasta was cooked. Add the pasta and toss over a medium heat until it is evenly coated. Pour in the sauce, toss lightly with two forks to mix with the pasta and heat through. Serve immediately, sprinkled with fresh herbs.

cook's tips
Parma ham is quite expensive but it tastes superb in this dish.
To cut the cost you could use ordinary cooked ham or pancetta.
If you can't get pipe rigate, use conchiglie or orecchiette instead,
both of which trap the peas.

ingredients

25g/1oz/2 tbsp **butter**
15ml/1 tbsp **olive oil**
150–175g/5–6oz/1¼–1½ cups
 frozen peas, thawed
1 **garlic** clove, crushed
150ml/¼ pint/⅔ cup **chicken
 stock**, **dry white wine**
 or **water**
30ml/2 tbsp chopped fresh **flat
 leaf parsley**
175ml/6fl oz/¾ cup **panna da
 cucina** or **double cream**
115g/4oz **Parma ham**, shredded
350g/12oz/3 cups dried
 pipe rigate
salt and freshly ground
 black pepper
chopped fresh **herbs**, to garnish

ingredients

225g/8oz dried **tagliatelle**

75–90g/3–3½oz **pancetta** or
   rindless **streaky bacon**, diced

25g/1oz/2 tbsp **butter**

1 **onion**, finely chopped

1 **garlic** clove, crushed

1 head of **radicchio**, about
   115–175g/4–6oz,
   finely shredded

150ml/¼ pint/⅔ cup **panna da
   cucina** or **double cream**

50g/2oz/⅔ cup freshly grated
   Parmesan cheese

salt and freshly ground
   black pepper

tagliatelle with radicchio & cream

THIS IS A **MODERN** RECIPE THAT IS VERY **QUICK** AND **EASY** TO MAKE. IT IS DELICIOUSLY **RICH**, AND MAKES A **GOOD DINNER PARTY** FIRST COURSE.

method

SERVES 4

1 Cook the pasta in a large saucepan of lightly salted boiling water for 8–10 minutes, until tender but still firm to the bite.

2 Meanwhile, put the pancetta or bacon in a medium saucepan and heat gently until the fat runs. Increase the heat slightly and stir-fry the pancetta or bacon for 5 minutes.

3 Add the butter, onion and garlic to the pan and stir-fry for 5 minutes more. Add the radicchio and toss for 1–2 minutes until wilted.

4 Pour in the cream and add the grated Parmesan, with salt and pepper to taste. Stir for 1–2 minutes until the cream is bubbling and the ingredients are evenly mixed. Taste for seasoning.

5 Drain the pasta and tip it into a warmed bowl. Pour the sauce over and toss well. Serve immediately.

cook's tip

In Italy, cooks use a variety of radicchio called radicchio di Treviso. It is very striking in appearance, with long leaves that are dramatically striped in dark red and white. Radicchio di Treviso is available in some supermarkets and specialist greengrocers, but if you cannot get it you can use the round radicchio instead.

fettuccine all' alfredo

THIS **SIMPLE** RECIPE WAS **INVENTED** BY A **ROMAN RESTAURATEUR** CALLED **ALFREDO**, WHO BECAME **FAMOUS** FOR SERVING IT WITH A **GOLDEN FORK** AND **SPOON**.

method

SERVES 4

1 Melt the butter in a large saucepan or frying pan. Add the cream and bring to the boil. Simmer, stirring constantly, for 5 minutes. Add the Parmesan, with salt and pepper to taste, and then turn off the heat under the pan.

2 Bring a large saucepan of lightly salted water to the boil. Drop in the pasta all at once and quickly bring back to the boil, stirring occasionally. Cook for 2–3 minutes, or until tender but still firm to the bite. Drain well.

3 Turn on the heat under the pan of cream to low, add the pasta all at once and toss until it is thoroughly coated in the sauce. Taste for seasoning. Serve immediately, with black pepper and extra grated Parmesan handed around separately.

---

cook's tips

With so few ingredients, it is particularly important to use only the best-quality ones for this dish to be a success. Use good unsalted butter and top-quality Parmesan cheese. The best is Parmigiano-Reggiano – available from Italian delicatessens – which has its name stamped on the rind. Grate it only just before using.

Fresh fettuccine is traditional, so either make it yourself or buy it from an Italian delicatessen. If you cannot get fettuccine, you can use tagliatelle instead.

---

ingredients

50g/2oz/¼ cup **butter**

200ml/7fl oz/scant 1 cup **panna da cucina** or **double cream**

50g/2oz/⅔ cup freshly grated **Parmesan cheese**, plus extra to serve

350g/12oz fresh **fettuccine**

salt and freshly ground **black pepper**

ingredients

350g/12oz dried **vermicelli**

juice of 2 large **lemons**

50g/2oz/4 tbsp **butter**

200ml/7fl oz/scant 1 cup **panna da cucina** or **double cream**

115g/4oz/1⅓ cups freshly grated **Parmesan cheese**

salt and freshly ground **black pepper**

lemon rind, to garnish

cook's tip

Lemons vary in the amount of juice they yield. On average, a large fresh lemon will yield 60–90ml/4–6 tbsp. The lemony flavour of this dish is quite sharp – you can use less juice if you prefer.

variations

Use spaghettini or spaghetti, or even small pasta shapes, such as fusilli, farfalle or orecchiette. For an even tangier taste, add a little grated lemon rind to the sauce when you add the butter and the cream to the pan in step 2.

vermicelli with lemon

FRESH AND **TANGY**, THIS DISH MAKES AN EXCELLENT **FIRST COURSE** FOR A DINNER PARTY. IT DOESN'T RELY ON FRESH SEASONAL INGREDIENTS SO IT IS A **GOOD** CHOICE AT **ANY TIME** OF **YEAR**. IT IS ALSO A **RECIPE** TO REMEMBER WHEN YOU'RE **PUSHED** FOR **TIME**, BECAUSE THE **SAUCE** CAN EASILY BE MADE IN THE **TIME** IT TAKES TO **COOK** THE **PASTA**.

method

SERVES 4

1 Cook the pasta in lightly salted boiling water for 8–10 minutes, until tender but still firm to the bite.

2 Meanwhile, pour the lemon juice into a medium saucepan. Add the butter and cream and season with salt and pepper to taste. Bring to the boil, then lower the heat and simmer for about 5 minutes, stirring occasionally, until the cream reduces slightly.

3 Drain the pasta and return it to the pan. Add the grated Parmesan, then taste the sauce for seasoning and pour it over the pasta. Toss quickly over a medium heat until the pasta is evenly coated with the sauce, then divide among four warmed bowls and serve immediately, garnished with lemon rind.

fusilli with wild mushrooms

A VERY **RICH DISH** WITH AN **EARTHY FLAVOUR** AND LOTS OF **GARLIC**, THIS MAKES AN IDEAL **MAIN COURSE** FOR **VEGETARIANS**, ESPECIALLY IF IT IS **FOLLOWED** BY A **CRISP GREEN SALAD**.

ingredients

½ x 275g/10oz jar **wild mushrooms** in olive oil
25g/1oz/2 tbsp **butter**
225g/8oz/2 cups fresh **wild mushrooms**, thinly sliced
5ml/1 tsp finely chopped fresh **thyme**
5ml/1 tsp finely chopped fresh **marjoram** or **oregano**, plus extra to serve
4 **garlic** cloves, crushed
350g/12oz/3 cups fresh or dried **fusilli**
200ml/7fl oz/scant 1 cup **panna da cucina** or **double cream**
salt and freshly ground **black pepper**

method

SERVES 4

1 Drain about 15ml/1 tbsp of the oil from the mushrooms into a medium saucepan. Slice or chop the bottled mushrooms into bite-size pieces, if they are large.

2 Add the butter to the oil in the pan and place over a low heat until sizzling. Add the bottled and the fresh mushrooms, the chopped herbs and the garlic, with salt and pepper to taste. Simmer over a medium heat, stirring frequently, for about 10 minutes, or until the fresh mushrooms are soft and tender.

3 Meanwhile, cook the pasta in lightly salted boiling water for about 2–3 minutes, if fresh, or 8–10 minutes, if dried, until tender but still firm to the bite.

4 As soon as the mushrooms are cooked, increase the heat to high and toss the mixture with a wooden spoon to drive off any excess liquid. Pour in the cream and bring to the boil, stirring, then taste and add more salt and pepper if needed.

5 Drain the pasta and tip it into a warmed bowl. Pour the sauce over the pasta and toss well. Serve immediately, sprinkled with finely chopped fresh herbs.

A LOVELY RECIPE FOR **LATE SPRING** WHEN BUNCHES OF **FRESH** YOUNG **ASPARAGUS** ARE **ON SALE** IN SHOPS AND MARKETS **EVERYWHERE**.

ingredients

250–300g/9–11oz fresh young
  asparagus
350g/12oz/3 cups dried
  garganelli
25g/1oz/2 tbsp **butter**
200ml/7fl oz/scant 1 cup **panna**
  da cucina or **double cream**
30ml/2 tbsp **dry white wine**
90–115g/3½–4oz/
  1–1⅓ cups freshly grated
  Parmesan cheese
30ml/2 tbsp chopped fresh
  mixed herbs, such as basil,
  flat leaf parsley and oregano
salt and freshly ground
  black pepper

garganelli with asparagus & cream

method

SERVES 4

1 Trim off and discard the woody ends of the asparagus – after trimming, you should have about 200g/7oz asparagus spears. Cut the spears diagonally into pieces that are roughly the same length and shape as the garganelli.

2 Blanch the asparagus spears in salted boiling water for 2 minutes, the tips for 1 minute. Immediately after blanching drain the asparagus spears and tips, rinse in cold water and set aside.

3 Cook the pasta in lightly salted boiling water for 8–10 minutes, until tender but still firm to the bite.

4 Meanwhile, put the butter and cream in a medium saucepan, add salt and pepper to taste and bring to the boil. Simmer for a few minutes until the cream reduces and thickens, then add the asparagus, wine and about half the grated Parmesan. Taste for seasoning and keep on a low heat.

5 Drain the pasta when cooked and tip it into a warmed bowl. Pour the sauce over the pasta, sprinkle with the fresh herbs and toss well. Serve immediately, topped with the remaining grated Parmesan and freshly ground black pepper, if liked.

cook's tips

When buying asparagus, look for thin stalks which will be sweet and tender. Don't buy asparagus with thick or woody stalks, which will be tough.
Garganelli all'uovo (with egg) are just perfect for this dish. You can buy packets of this pasta in Italian delicatessens.
Penne (quills) or penne rigate (ridged quills) are an alternative pasta for this recipe. They are similar in shape and size to garganelli.

spaghetti carbonara

AN **ALL-TIME FAVOURITE** THAT NEEDS NO INTRODUCTION. THIS **VERSION** HAS PLENTY OF **PANCETTA** OR BACON AND IS **NOT TOO CREAMY**, BUT YOU CAN **VARY** THE AMOUNTS AS YOU **PLEASE**.

method

SERVES 4

1 Heat the oil in a large saucepan or frying pan, add the finely chopped onion and cook over a low heat, stirring frequently, for about 5 minutes until softened but not coloured.

2 Add the strips of pancetta or bacon to the onion in the pan and cook, stirring very frequently, for about 10 minutes.

3 Meanwhile, cook the pasta in a pan of salted boiling water for 2–3 minutes, if fresh, or 8–10 minutes, if dried, until tender but still firm to the bite.

4 Put the eggs, crème fraîche and grated Parmesan in a bowl. Grind in plenty of pepper, then beat everything together well.

5 Drain the pasta, tip it into the pan with the pancetta or bacon and toss well to mix. Turn the heat off under the pan. Immediately add the egg mixture and toss vigorously so that it cooks very lightly and coats the pasta.

6 Quickly taste for seasoning, then divide among four warmed bowls and sprinkle with black pepper. Serve immediately, with extra grated Parmesan served separately.

ingredients

30ml/2 tbsp **olive oil**

1 small **onion**, finely chopped

8 rashers of **pancetta** or rindless **smoked streaky bacon**, cut into 1cm/½in strips

350g/12oz fresh or dried **spaghetti**

4 **eggs**

60ml/4 tbsp **crème fraîche**

60ml/4 tbsp freshly grated **Parmesan cheese**, plus extra to serve

salt and freshly ground **black pepper**

light suppers

rigatoni with winter tomato sauce

IN **WINTER**, WHEN **FRESH TOMATOES** ARE NOT AT THEIR **BEST**, THIS IS THE **SAUCE** THE **ITALIANS** MAKE. CANNED TOMATOES COMBINED WITH **SOFFRITO** (THE SAUTEED MIXTURE OF CHOPPED ONION, CARROT, CELERY AND GARLIC) AND **HERBS** GIVE A **BETTER FLAVOUR** THAN WINTER TOMATOES.

method

SERVES 6–8

1 Finely chop the onion, carrot and celery stick, either in a food processor or with a sharp knife.

2 Heat the olive oil in a medium saucepan, add the garlic slices and stir over a very low heat for 1–2 minutes.

3 Add the chopped vegetables and the fresh herbs. Cook over a low heat, stirring frequently, for 5–7 minutes, until the vegetables have softened and are lightly coloured.

4 Add the canned tomatoes, tomato paste and sugar, then stir in the wine, if using. Add salt and pepper to taste. Bring to the boil, stirring, then lower the heat to a gentle simmer. Cook, uncovered, for about 45 minutes, stirring occasionally.

5 Cook the pasta in lightly salted boiling water for 8–10 minutes, until tender, but still firm to the bite. Drain it and tip it into a warmed bowl. Taste the sauce for seasoning, pour the sauce over the pasta and toss well. Serve immediately, with shavings of Parmesan served separately. If you like, garnish with extra chopped herbs.

ingredients

1 **onion**
1 **carrot**
1 **celery** stick
60ml/4 tbsp **olive oil**
1 **garlic** clove, thinly sliced
a few leaves each fresh **basil**,
   thyme and **oregano**
   or **marjoram**
2 x 400g/14oz cans chopped
   plum tomatoes
15ml/1 tbsp **sun-dried**
   tomato paste
5ml/1 tsp **sugar**
about 90ml/6 tbsp **dry red** or
   white wine (optional)
350g/12oz/3 cups dried **rigatoni**
salt and freshly ground
   black pepper
coarsely shaved **Parmesan**
   cheese, to serve

ingredients

350g/12oz skinless **chicken**
   breast fillets, cut into bite-
   size pieces
60ml/4 tbsp **Italian dry**
   vermouth
10ml/2 tsp chopped fresh
   rosemary, plus 4 fresh
   rosemary sprigs, to garnish
15ml/1 tbsp **olive oil**
1 **onion**, finely chopped
90g/3½oz piece **Italian**
   salami, diced
275g/10oz/2½ cups
   dried **farfalle**
15ml/1 tbsp **balsamic vinegar**
400g/14oz can **Italian**
   cherry tomatoes
good pinch of crushed **dried**
   red chillies
salt and freshly ground
   black pepper

cook's tip
The tomatoes look good left whole,
but if you prefer you can crush them
with the back of a wooden spoon
while they are simmering in the pan.

farfalle with chicken & cherry tomatoes

QUICK TO **PREPARE** AND EASY TO COOK,
THIS **COLOURFUL** DISH IS **FULL** OF
FLAVOUR. SERVE IT FOR A MIDWEEK
SUPPER, WITH A **GREEN SALAD** TO FOLLOW.

method   SERVES 4

1 Put the pieces of chicken in a large bowl, pour in the dry vermouth
   and sprinkle with half the chopped rosemary and salt and pepper to
   taste. Stir well and set aside.

2 Heat the oil in a large frying pan, add the onion and salami and fry
   over a medium heat, stirring frequently, for about 5 minutes.

3 Cook the pasta in lightly salted boiling water for 8–10 minutes, until
   tender but still firm to the bite.

4 Add the chicken and vermouth to the onion and salami, increase the
   heat to high and fry for 3 minutes, or until the chicken is white on all
   sides. Sprinkle the vinegar over the chicken. Add the cherry tomatoes
   and dried chillies. Stir well and simmer for a few minutes more. Taste
   the sauce for seasoning.

5 Drain the pasta and tip it into the frying pan. Add the remaining
   chopped rosemary and toss thoroughly to mix the pasta and sauce
   together. Serve immediately in warmed bowls, garnished with the
   rosemary sprigs.

spaghetti with saffron

method

1 Cook the pasta in a saucepan of lightly salted boiling water for 8–10 minutes, until tender but still firm to the bite.

2 Meanwhile, put the saffron strands in a saucepan, add the water and bring to the boil immediately. Remove the pan from the heat and leave to stand for a while.

3 Add the strips of ham to the pan containing the saffron. Stir in the cream and Parmesan, with a little salt and pepper to taste. Heat gently, stirring constantly. When the cream starts to bubble around the edges, remove the sauce from the heat and add the egg yolks. Beat well to mix, then taste for seasoning.

4 Drain the pasta and tip it into a warmed bowl. Immediately pour the sauce over the pasta and toss well. Serve immediately, with extra grated Parmesan handed separately.

A **DELICIOUS**, QUICK AND EASY DISH THAT IS PERFECT FOR A **MIDWEEK SUPPER**. THE INGREDIENTS ARE ALL **STAPLES** THAT YOU ARE VERY **LIKELY** TO HAVE IN THE **FRIDGE**, SO THIS RECIPE IS **PERFECT** FOR **IMPROMPTU** MEALS.

ingredients

350g/12oz dried **spaghetti**

a few **saffron strands**

30ml/2 tbsp **water**

150g/5oz **cooked ham**, cut into matchsticks

200ml/7fl oz/scant 1 cup **panna da cucina** or **double cream**

50g/2oz/⅔ cup freshly grated **Parmesan cheese**, plus extra to serve

2 **egg yolks**

salt and freshly ground **black pepper**

cook's tips

Individual sachets of saffron powder, enough for four servings, are sold at Italian delicatessens and some supermarkets, and one sachet can be used for this sauce instead of the saffron strands. Simply sprinkle in the powder in step 3, when adding salt and pepper.

Use a heavy-based pan for heating the cream so that it does not catch on the bottom. Make sure you beat the sauce immediately the eggs have been added.

ingredients

30ml/2 tbsp **olive oil**

1 small **onion**, finely chopped

1 **garlic** clove, finely chopped

400g/14oz can chopped **Italian
plum tomatoes**

45ml/3 tbsp **dry white wine**

8–10 pitted black **olives**,
cut into rings

10ml/2 tsp chopped fresh
oregano or 5ml/1 tsp **dried
oregano**, plus extra fresh
oregano to garnish

400g/14oz/3½ cups dried
farfalle

175g/6oz can **tuna** in olive oil

salt and freshly ground
black pepper

variation
For a more intense flavour, add
two or three drained bottled
anchovy fillets when frying the
onion and garlic.

farfalle with tuna

A **QUICK** AND **SIMPLE** DISH THAT MAKES
A GOOD **WEEKDAY SUPPER** IF YOU HAVE
CANNED **TOMATOES** AND **TUNA** IN THE
STORE CUPBOARD.

method   SERVES 4

1 Heat the olive oil in a medium skillet or saucepan, add the onion
and garlic and fry gently for 2–3 minutes until the onion is soft
and golden.

2 Add the plum tomatoes and bring to the boil, then add the white wine
and simmer for a minute or so. Stir in the olives and oregano, with salt
and pepper to taste, then cover and cook for 20–25 minutes, stirring
from time to time.

3 Meanwhile, cook the pasta in a large saucepan of salted boiling water
according to the instructions on the packet.

4 Drain the canned tuna and flake it with a fork. Add the tuna to the
sauce with about 60ml/4 tbsp of the water used for cooking the
pasta. Taste and adjust the seasoning.

5 Drain the cooked pasta well and tip it into a warmed large serving
bowl. Pour the tuna sauce over the top and toss to mix. Serve
immediately, garnished with sprigs of oregano.

penne with tomato & chilli sauce

THIS IS ONE OF **ROME'S** MOST **FAMOUS** PASTA **DISHES** – PENNE TOSSED IN A TOMATO SAUCE **FLAVOURED** WITH **CHILLI**. LITERALLY TRANSLATED, ITS ITALIAN NAME, **ARRABBIATA**, MEANS **ENRAGED** OR FURIOUS, BUT IN THIS CONTEXT IT SHOULD BE TRANSLATED AS **FIERY**. MAKE THE SAUCE AS **HOT** AS YOU LIKE BY **ADDING** MORE **CHILLIES** TO TASTE.

method

SERVES 4

1 Soak the dried mushrooms in sufficient warm water to cover for 15–20 minutes. Drain, then squeeze dry with your hands. Finely chop the mushrooms.

2 Melt 50g/2oz/4 tbsp of the butter in a medium saucepan or frying pan. Add the pancetta or bacon and stir-fry over a medium heat until golden and slightly crispy. Remove with a slotted spoon and set aside.

3 Add the chopped mushrooms to the pan and cook in the same way. Remove and set aside with the pancetta or bacon. Crumble 1 chilli into the pan, add the garlic and cook, stirring, for a few minutes, until the garlic turns golden.

4 Add the tomatoes and basil and season with salt. Cook gently, stirring occasionally, for 10–15 minutes.

5 Meanwhile, cook the penne in lightly salted boiling water for 2–3 minutes, if fresh, or 8–10 minutes, if dried, until tender but still firm to the bite.

6 Add the pancetta or bacon and the mushrooms to the tomato sauce. Taste for seasoning, adding more chillies if you prefer a hotter flavour. If the sauce is too dry, stir in a little of the pasta water.

7 Drain the pasta and tip it into a warmed bowl. Dice the remaining butter, add it to the pasta with the cheeses, then toss until well coated. Pour the tomato sauce over the pasta, toss well and serve immediately with a few basil leaves sprinkled on top.

ingredients

25g/1oz dried **porcini mushrooms**

90g/3½oz/7 tbsp **butter**

150g/5oz **pancetta** or rindless **smoked streaky bacon**, diced

1–2 dried **red chillies**, to taste

2 **garlic** cloves, crushed

8 ripe **plum tomatoes**, peeled and chopped

a few fresh **basil leaves**, torn, plus extra to garnish

350g/12oz/3 cups fresh or dried **penne**

50g/2oz/⅔ cup freshly grated **Parmesan cheese**

25g/1oz/⅓ cup freshly grated **Pecorino cheese**

salt

ingredients

60ml/4 tbsp **olive oil**

1 **garlic** clove, roughly chopped

450g/1lb ripe **plum tomatoes**,
    peeled and chopped

vegetable oil, for shallow-frying

350g/12oz **aubergines**,
    finely diced

400g/14oz fresh or dried
    spaghetti

1 handful fresh **basil leaves**,
    shredded

115g/4oz **ricotta salata
    cheese**, coarsely grated

salt and freshly ground
    black pepper

spaghetti with aubergines

CALLED **SPAGHETTI BELLINI** IN ITALY,
THIS FAMOUS DISH IS **NAMED** AFTER THE
SICILIAN COMPOSER. YOU MAY ALSO
COME ACROSS IT CALLED **SPAGHETTI ALLA
NORMA** AFTER HIS FAMOUS **OPERA**.

method

SERVES 4–6

1 Heat the olive oil in a large saucepan, add the garlic and cook over
a low heat, stirring constantly, for 1–2 minutes. Stir in the chopped
tomatoes and season with salt and pepper to taste. Cover and simmer
for 20 minutes.

2 Meanwhile, pour vegetable oil into a deep, heavy-based frying pan to
a depth of about 1cm/½in. Heat the oil until it is hot but not smoking.
Add the aubergine cubes, in batches if necessary, and fry for about
4–5 minutes, until tender and lightly browned all over.

3 Remove the aubergine cubes with a slotted spoon and drain
thoroughly on absorbent kitchen paper.

4 Cook the spaghetti in lightly salted boiling water for 2–3 minutes, if
fresh, or 8–10 minutes, if dried, until tender but still firm to the bite.

5 Meanwhile, stir the fried aubergines cubes into the tomato sauce and
warm through. Taste for seasoning.

6 Drain the pasta thoroughly and tip it into a warmed bowl. Add the
sauce, with the shredded basil and a generous handful of the grated
ricotta salata. Toss well to coat and serve immediately, with the
remaining ricotta sprinkled on top.

sugo di verdure

ALTHOUGH DESCRIBED AS "**SUGO**" IN **ITALIAN**, THIS IS NOT A **TRUE SAUCE** BECAUSE IT DOES NOT HAVE ANY **LIQUID** APART FROM THE **OIL** AND **MELTED BUTTER**. IT IS MORE A **MEDLEY** OF **VEGETABLES**, WHICH CAN BE **VARIED** ACCORDING TO THE **SEASON**. TOSSED WITH ABOUT 450G/1LB FRESHLY COOKED PASTA, IT IS **IDEAL** FOR A **FRESH** AND **LIGHT LUNCH** OR **SUPPER**.

ingredients

2 **carrots**

1 **courgette**

75g/3oz **French beans**

1 small **leek**

2 ripe **plum tomatoes**

1 handful fresh **flat leaf parsley**

25g/1oz/2 tbsp **butter**

45ml/3 tbsp extra virgin **olive oil**

2.5ml/½ tsp **sugar**

115g/4oz/1 cup **frozen peas**

salt and freshly ground
   black pepper

method

SERVES 4

1 Finely dice the carrots and the courgette. Top and tail the French beans, then cut them into 2cm/¾in lengths. Slice the leek thinly. Peel and dice the tomatoes. Chop the flat leaf parsley and set aside.

2 Heat the butter with the oil in a medium frying pan or saucepan. When the mixture sizzles, add the prepared leek and carrots. Sprinkle the sugar over and fry, stirring frequently, for about 5 minutes.

3 Stir in the courgette, French beans, peas and plenty of salt and pepper. Cover and cook over a low to medium heat, stirring occasionally, for 5–8 minutes, until the vegetables are tender.

4 Stir in the chopped plum tomatoes and parsley and adjust the seasoning to taste. Serve at once, tossed with freshly cooked pasta of your choice.

frittata di vermicelli

A FRITTATA IS A **FLAT BAKED** OMELETTE. HERE IT IS MADE WITH **VEGETABLES** AND HERBS BUT YOU CAN ADD **ANYTHING** YOU **FANCY** TO IT. HAM, SAUSAGE, **SALAMI**, CHICKEN, **MUSHROOMS**, COURGETTES AND AUBERGINES ARE JUST A FEW **SUGGESTIONS**, OR YOU COULD **SIMPLY** ADD MIXED HERBS. FRITTATA IS ABSOLUTELY DELICIOUS **COLD**. CUT INTO **WEDGES**, IT MAKES EXCELLENT FOOD FOR **PICNICS**.

method

SERVES 4–6

1 Preheat the oven to 190ºC/375ºF/Gas 5. Cook the pasta in salted boiling water for 8–10 minutes, until tender but still firm to the bite.

2 Meanwhile, break the eggs into a bowl and add the cream and herbs. Whisk in about two-thirds of the grated Parmesan and add salt and pepper to taste.

3 Drain the pasta well and allow it to cool, then snip it into short lengths with scissors. Add to the egg mixture and whisk again. Set aside.

4 Heat the butter with the oil in a large, ovenproof non-stick frying pan. Add the onion and cook gently, stirring frequently, for 5 minutes, until softened. Add the peppers and garlic.

5 Pour the egg and pasta mixture into the pan and stir well. Cook over a low to medium heat, without stirring, for 3–5 minutes, or until the frittata is just set underneath. Sprinkle over the remaining Parmesan and bake in the oven for 5 minutes, or until set. Before serving, leave to stand for at least 5 minutes. Cut into wedges and serve warm or cold, with rocket.

ingredients

50g/2oz dried **vermicelli**

6 **eggs**

60ml/4 tbsp **panna da cucina** or **double cream**

1 handful fresh **basil leaves**, shredded

1 handful fresh **flat leaf parsley**, chopped

75g/3oz/1 cup freshly grated **Parmesan cheese**

25g/1oz/2 tbsp **butter**

15ml/1 tbsp **olive oil**

1 **onion**, finely sliced

3 large pieces **bottled roasted red pepper**, drained, rinsed, dried and cut into strips

1 **garlic** clove, crushed

salt and freshly ground **black pepper**

rocket leaves, to serve.

ingredients

250g/9oz/2¼ cups dried **elbow macaroni**

50g/2oz/4 tbsp **butter**

50g/2oz/½ cup **flour**

600ml/1 pint/2½ cups **milk**

100ml/3½ fl oz/scant ½ cup **panna da cucina** or **double cream**

100ml/3½ fl oz/scant ½ cup **dry white wine**

50g/2oz/½ cup grated **Gruyère** or **Emmenthal cheese**

50g/2oz **fontina cheese**, diced small

50g/2oz **Gorgonzola cheese**, crumbled

75g/3oz/1 cup freshly grated **Parmesan cheese**

salt and freshly ground **black pepper**

rocket leaves, to serve

macaroni with four cheeses

RICH AND CREAMY, THIS IS A **DE LUXE MACARONI CHEESE** THAT CAN BE SERVED FOR AN **INFORMAL LUNCH** OR SUPPER **PARTY**. IT GOES WELL WITH EITHER A **TOMATO** AND **BASIL SALAD** OR A **LEAFY** GREEN **SALAD**.

method

SERVES 4

1 Preheat the oven to 180°C/350°F/Gas 4. Cook the pasta in salted boiling water for 8–10 minutes, until tender but still firm to the bite.

2 Meanwhile, melt the butter in a medium saucepan, add the flour and cook, stirring, for 1–2 minutes. Add the milk a little at a time, whisking vigorously after each addition. Stir in the cream, followed by the dry white wine. Bring to the boil. Cook, stirring constantly, until the sauce thickens, then remove the pan from the heat.

3 Add the Gruyère or Emmenthal, fontina, Gorgonzola and about a third of the grated Parmesan to the sauce. Stir well to mix in the cheeses, then taste for seasoning and add salt and pepper if necessary.

4 Drain the pasta and tip it into an ovenproof dish. Pour the sauce over the pasta, mix well and sprinkle the remaining Parmesan over the top. Bake for 25–30 minutes, or until golden brown. Serve hot.

cook's tip
Fontina is a mountain cheese with a slightly sweet, nutty flavour. If you can't get it, use Taleggio instead or double the quantity of Gruyère or Emmenthal.

fish & shellfish

seafood conchiglie

THIS **WARM SALAD** IS COMPOSED OF **SCALLOPS**, PASTA AND **ROCKET** FLAVOURED WITH **ROASTED PEPPER**, CHILLI AND BALSAMIC VINEGAR. IT MAKES AN **IMPRESSIVE DINNER PARTY** STARTER OR A MAIN COURSE FOR A **LIGHT LUNCH**.

method

SERVES 4

1 Cut each scallop into 2–3 pieces. If the corals are attached, pull them off and cut each one in half. Season the scallops and corals with salt and pepper.

2 To make the vinaigrette, put the oil, vinegar, chopped pepper and chillies in a jug with the garlic and honey and whisk well.

3 Cook the pasta in lightly salted boiling water for 8–10 minutes, until tender but still firm to the bite.

4 Meanwhile, heat the oil and butter in a non-stick frying pan until sizzling. Add half the scallops and toss over a high heat for 2 minutes. Remove with a slotted spoon and keep warm. Cook the remaining scallops in the same way.

5 Add the wine to the liquid remaining in the pan and stir over a high heat until the mixture has reduced to a few tablespoons. Remove from the heat and keep warm.

6 Drain the pasta and tip it into a warmed bowl. Add the rocket, scallops, the reduced cooking juices and the vinaigrette and toss well to combine. Serve immediately.

cook's tips

Use only fresh scallops for this dish – they are available all year round in most fishmongers and from fish counters in supermarkets. Frozen scallops tend to be watery and tasteless and often prove to be rubbery when cooked.
For a more formal presentation, arrange the rocket leaves in a circle on each of four individual serving plates. Toss the pasta, scallops, reduced cooking juices and vinaigrette together and spoon into the centre of the rocket leaves.

ingredients

8 large fresh **scallops**
300g/11oz/2¾ cups dried **conchiglie**
15ml/1 tbsp **olive oil**
15g/½oz/1 tbsp **butter**
120ml/4fl oz/½ cup **dry white wine**
90g/3½oz **rocket leaves**, stalks trimmed
salt and freshly ground **black pepper**

For the vinaigrette
60ml/4 tbsp extra virgin **olive oil**
15ml/1 tbsp **balsamic vinegar**
1 piece **bottled roasted pepper**, drained and finely chopped
1–2 fresh **red chillies**, seeded and chopped
1 **garlic** clove, crushed
5–10ml/1–2 tsp **clear honey**

ingredients

45ml/3 tbsp **olive oil**

1 small **onion**, finely chopped

1 **garlic** clove, crushed

½ fresh **red chilli**, seeded
   and chopped

200g/7oz can chopped
   plum tomatoes

30ml/2 tbsp chopped fresh
   flat leaf parsley

400g/14oz fresh **clams**

400g/14oz fresh **mussels**

60ml/4 tbsp **dry white wine**

400g/14oz dried **trenette**

a few fresh **basil leaves**

90g/3½oz/⅔ cup peeled cooked
   prawns, thawed and
   thoroughly dried, if frozen

salt and freshly ground
   black pepper

chopped **fresh herbs**, to garnish

lemon wedges, to serve

trenette with shellfish

COLOURFUL AND DELICIOUS, THIS **TYPICAL** GENOESE DISH IS **IDEAL** FOR A **DINNER PARTY**. THE SAUCE IS QUITE RUNNY, SO SERVE IT WITH FRESH **CRUSTY BREAD** AND **SPOONS** AS WELL AS FORKS.

method

SERVES 4

1 Heat 30ml/2 tbsp of the oil in a frying pan or medium saucepan. Add the onion, garlic and chilli and cook over a medium heat, stirring constantly, for 1–2 minutes. Stir in the tomatoes, half the parsley and pepper to taste. Bring to the boil, lower the heat, cover and simmer for 15 minutes.

2 Meanwhile, scrub the clams and mussels under cold running water. Discard any that are open or that do not close when sharply tapped against the work surface.

3 In a large saucepan, heat the remaining oil. Add the clams and mussels, with the remaining parsley and toss over a high heat for a few seconds. Pour in the wine, cover tightly and cook for about 5 minutes, shaking the pan frequently, until the clams and mussels have opened.

4 Remove the pan from the heat and transfer the clams and mussels to a bowl with a slotted spoon, discarding any that remain closed.

5 Strain the cooking liquid into a measuring jug and set aside. Reserve four or eight clams and four mussels in their shells for the garnish, then remove the rest from their shells.

6 Cook the pasta in lightly salted boiling water for 8–10 minutes, until tender but still firm to the bite.

7 Meanwhile, add 120ml/4fl oz/½ cup of the reserved seafood liquid to the tomato sauce. Bring to the boil over a high heat, stirring. Lower the heat, tear in the basil leaves and add the prawns with the shelled clams and mussels. Stir well, then taste for seasoning.

8 Drain the pasta and tip it into a warmed bowl. Add the seafood sauce and toss well. Serve in individual bowls, sprinkle with herbs and garnish with the reserved clams and mussels in their shells and lemon.

THIS IS A GOOD DISH TO **MAKE** IN **LATE SPRING** OR **EARLY SUMMER**, WHEN GREENY-PURPLE **BABY ARTICHOKES** APPEAR IN **SHOPS** AND ON MARKET **STALLS**.

ingredients

juice of ½ **lemon**

4 baby globe **artichokes**

90ml/6 tbsp **olive oil**

2 **garlic** cloves, crushed

30ml/2 tbsp chopped fresh **mint**

30ml/2 tbsp chopped fresh **flat leaf parsley**

350g/12oz/3 cups dried **penne**

8–12 peeled cooked **king** or **tiger prawns**, each cut into 2–3 pieces

25g/1oz/2 tbsp **butter**

salt and freshly ground **black pepper**

penne with prawns & artichokes

method

SERVES 4

1 Have ready a bowl of cold water to which you have added the lemon juice. To prepare the artichokes, cut off the artichoke stalks, if any, and cut across the tops of the leaves. Peel off and discard any tough or discoloured outer leaves.

2 Cut the artichokes lengthways into quarters and remove any hairy chokes from their centres. Finally, cut the pieces of artichoke lengthways into 5mm/¼in slices and put these in the bowl of acidulated water.

3 Drain the slices of artichoke and pat them dry. Heat the olive oil in a non-stick frying pan and add the artichokes, the crushed garlic and half the mint and parsley.

4 Season with plenty of salt and pepper. Cook over a low heat, stirring frequently, for about 10 minutes, or until the artichokes feel tender when pierced with a sharp knife.

5 Meanwhile, cook the pasta in lightly salted boiling water for about 8–10 minutes, until tender but still firm to the bite.

6 Add the prawns to the artichokes, stir well to mix, then heat through gently for 1–2 minutes.

7 Drain the pasta and tip it into a warmed bowl. Add the butter and toss until it has melted. Spoon the artichoke mixture over the pasta and toss to combine. Serve immediately, sprinkled with the remaining fresh herbs.

linguine with crab

THIS RECIPE COMES FROM **ROME**. IT MAKES A **VERY RICH** AND TASTY FIRST COURSE ON ITS OWN OR CAN BE **SERVED** FOR A LUNCH OR SUPPER WITH CRUSTY ITALIAN BREAD. **SOME COOKS** LIKE A **FINER SAUCE** AND WORK THE **CRAB MEAT** THROUGH A SIEVE AFTER POUNDING. IF YOU FANCY FOLLOWING THEIR EXAMPLE, **BE WARNED** – IT'S VERY HARD WORK.

method

SERVES 4

1 Put the crab meat in a mortar and pound to a rough pulp with a pestle. If you do not have a pestle and mortar, use a sturdy bowl and the end of a rolling pin. Set aside.

2 Heat 30ml/2 tbsp of the oil in a large saucepan. Add the parsley and garlic, with salt and pepper to taste, and fry for a few minutes until the garlic begins to brown.

3 Add the tomatoes, pounded crab meat and wine, cover the pan and simmer gently, stirring occasionally, for 15 minutes.

4 Meanwhile, cook the pasta in lightly salted boiling water for 2–3 minutes, if fresh, or 8–10 minutes, if dried, until tender but still firm to the bite. Drain and reserve a little of the cooking water.

5 Return the pasta to the clean pan, add the remaining oil and toss quickly over a medium heat until the oil coats the strands.

6 Add the tomato and crab mixture to the pasta and toss again, adding a little of the reserved cooking water if necessary. Adjust the seasoning to taste. Serve immediately, on warmed plates, sprinkled with parsley.

ingredients

about 250g/9oz shelled
   crab meat
45ml/3 tbsp **olive oil**
1 small handful fresh **flat leaf**
   parsley, roughly chopped,
   plus extra to garnish
1 **garlic** clove, crushed
350g/12oz ripe **plum tomatoes**,
   peeled and chopped
60–90ml/4–6 tbsp **dry**
   white wine
350g/12oz fresh or
   dried **linguine**
salt and freshly ground
   black pepper

cook's tip
The best way to obtain crab meat is to ask a fishmonger to remove it from the shell for you or to buy dressed crab from the supermarket. For this recipe you will need one large crab, and you should use both the white and dark meat.

tagliolini with clams & mussels

SERVED ON **WHITE CHINA**, THIS MAKES A **STUNNING DISH** FOR A DINNER PARTY FIRST COURSE. THE **SAUCE** CAN BE PREPARED A FEW HOURS AHEAD OF TIME, THEN THE **PASTA** COOKED AND THE DISH **ASSEMBLED** AT THE **LAST MINUTE**.

method

SERVES 4

1 Scrub the mussels and clams under cold running water and discard any that are open or damaged or that do not close when sharply tapped against the work surface.

2 Heat half the oil in a large saucepan, add the onion and cook gently for about 5 minutes, until softened. Sprinkle in the garlic, then add about half the parsley sprigs, with salt and pepper to taste. Add the mussels and clams and pour in the wine. Cover tightly and bring to the boil over a high heat. Cook, shaking the pan frequently, for about 5 minutes, until the shellfish have opened.

3 Tip the mussels and clams into a fine sieve set over a bowl and let the liquid drain through. Discard the aromatics in the sieve, together with any mussels or clams that have not opened. Return the liquid to the clean pan and add the fish stock. Finely chop the remaining parsley and add it to the liquid with the chopped chilli. Bring to the boil, then lower the heat and simmer, stirring, for a few minutes, until slightly reduced. Turn off the heat.

4 Remove and discard the top shells from about half the mussels and clams. Put all the mussels and clams in the pan of liquid and seasonings, then cover the pan tightly and set aside.

5 Cook the pasta in lightly salted boiling water for 2–3 minutes, if fresh, or 8–10 minutes, if dried, until tender but still firm to the bite.

6 Drain well, then return to the clean pan and toss with the remaining olive oil. Put the pan of shellfish over a high heat and toss to heat the shellfish through and combine with the liquid and seasonings.

7 Divide the pasta among four warmed plates, spoon the shellfish mixture over, then serve immediately, sprinkled with parsley.

ingredients

450g/1lb fresh **mussels**
450g/1lb fresh **clams**
60ml/4 tbsp **olive oil**
1 small **onion**, finely chopped
2 **garlic** cloves, finely chopped
1 large handful fresh **flat leaf parsley**, plus extra chopped parsley to garnish
175ml/6fl oz/¾ cup **dry white wine**
250ml/8fl oz/1 cup **fish stock**
1 small fresh **red chilli**, seeded and chopped
350g/12oz fresh or dried **squid ink tagliolini** or **tagliatelle**
salt and freshly ground **black pepper**

ingredients

meat from the body, tail and claws
of 1 **cooked lobster**

juice of ½ **lemon**

40g/1½oz/3 tbsp **butter**

4 fresh **tarragon sprigs**, leaves
stripped and chopped, plus
extra to garnish

60ml/4 tbsp **panna da cucina**
or **double cream**

90ml/6 tbsp **sparkling dry
white wine**

60ml/4 tbsp **fish stock**

300g/11oz fresh **capelli
d'angelo**

salt and freshly ground
black pepper

about 10ml/2 tsp **lumpfish roe**,
to garnish (optional)

capelli d'angelo with lobster

THIS IS A **SOPHISTICATED**, STYLISH DISH
FOR A **SPECIAL OCCASION**. SOME COOKS
MAKE THE **SAUCE** WITH **CHAMPAGNE**
RATHER THAN SPARKLING WHITE WINE,
ESPECIALLY WHEN THEY ARE PLANNING TO
SERVE CHAMPAGNE WITH **THE MEAL**.

method

SERVES 4

1 Cut the lobster meat into small pieces and put it in a bowl. Sprinkle
with the lemon juice. Melt the butter in a frying pan or large saucepan,
add the lobster meat and tarragon and stir for a few seconds. Add the
cream and stir for a few seconds more, then pour in the wine and
stock, with salt and pepper to taste. Simmer for 2 minutes, then
remove from the heat and cover.

2 Cook the pasta in lightly salted boiling water for 2–3 minutes, until
tender but still firm to the bite. Drain well, reserving a few spoonfuls of
the cooking water.

3 Place the pan of lobster sauce over a medium to high heat, add
the pasta and toss to combine and heat through, moistening with a
little of the reserved cooking water. Serve immediately in warmed
bowls, garnish with tarragon leaves and sprinkle with lumpfish roe,
if you like.

cook's tip

To remove the meat from a lobster, place the lobster on a board with
its underbelly facing uppermost. With a large sharp knife, cut the lobster in
half lengthways. Spoon out the green liver and any pink roe (coral) and
reserve them, then remove and discard the gravel sac (stomach). Pull
the white tail meat out from either side of the shell and discard the black
intestinal vein. Crack the claws with nutcrackers just below the pincers and
remove the meat from the base. Pull away the small pincer, taking the white
membrane with it, then remove the meat from this part of the shell.
Pull the meat from the large pincer shell.

ingredients

300g/11oz **salmon fillet**

200ml/7fl oz/scant 1 cup **dry white wine**

a few fresh **basil sprigs**, plus extra basil leaves, to garnish

6 ripe **plum tomatoes**, peeled and finely chopped

150ml/¼ pint/⅔ cup **panna da cucina** or **double cream**

350g/12oz fresh or dried **linguine**

115g/4oz/⅔ cup peeled cooked **prawns**, thawed if frozen

salt and freshly ground **black pepper**

linguine with salmon & prawns

THIS IS A LOVELY **FRESH-TASTING** PASTA DISH, PERFECT FOR AN **AL FRESCO** MEAL IN SUMMER. SERVE IT AS A MAIN COURSE FOR LUNCH WITH **WARM CIABATTA** OR FOCACCIA AND A **DRY WHITE WINE**.

method

SERVES 4

1 Put the salmon skin side up in a wide shallow pan. Pour the wine over, add the basil sprigs and sprinkle the fish with salt and pepper. Bring to the boil, cover and simmer gently for no more than 5 minutes. Lift the fish out of the pan with a fish slice and set aside to cool a little.

2 Add the tomatoes and cream to the liquid remaining in the pan and bring to the boil. Stir well, then lower the heat and simmer, uncovered, for 10–15 minutes. Meanwhile, cook the pasta in lightly salted boiling water for 2–3 minutes, if fresh, or 8–10 minutes, if dried, until tender but still firm to the bite.

3 Flake the fish into large chunks, discarding the skin and any bones. Add the fish to the sauce with the prawns, shaking the pan until the fish and shellfish are well coated. Taste for seasoning.

4 Drain the pasta and tip it into a warmed bowl. Pour the sauce over the pasta and toss to combine. Serve immediately, garnished with fresh basil leaves.

cook's tip
Check the salmon fillet carefully for small bones when you are flaking the flesh. Although the salmon is already filleted, you will always find a few stray "pin" bones. Pick them out carefully using tweezers or your fingertips.

fish with fregola

THIS **SARDINIAN SPECIALITY** IS A CROSS BETWEEN A **SOUP** AND A **STEW**. SERVE IT WITH CRUSTY ITALIAN **COUNTRY BREAD** TO **MOP UP** THE **JUICES**.

method

SERVES 4–6

1 Heat 30ml/2 tbsp of the olive oil in a large flameproof casserole. Add the chopped garlic and chilli, with about half the chopped fresh parsley. Fry over a medium heat, stirring occasionally, for about 5 minutes.

2 Cut all of the fish into large chunks – including the skin and the bones in the case of the snapper and mullet – and add the pieces to the casserole as you cut them. Sprinkle the pieces with a further 30ml/ 2 tbsp of the olive oil and fry for a few minutes more.

3 Add the tomatoes, then fill the empty can with water and pour this into the pan. Bring to the boil. Stir in salt and pepper to taste, lower the heat and cook for 10 minutes, stirring occasionally.

4 Add the fregola and simmer for 5 minutes, then add 250ml/8fl oz/ 1 cup water and the remaining oil. Simmer for 15 minutes until the fregola is tender but still firm to the bite.

5 If the sauce becomes too thick, add more water, then taste for seasoning. Serve hot, in warmed bowls, sprinkled with the remaining parsley.

cook's tips
You can make the basic fish sauce several hours in advance or even the day before, bringing it to the boil and adding the fregola just before serving. Fregola is a tiny pasta shape from Sardinia. If you can't get it, use a tiny soup pasta (pastina), such as corallini or semi de melone.

ingredients

75ml/5 tbsp **olive oil**

4 **garlic** cloves, finely chopped

½ small fresh **red chilli**, seeded and finely chopped

1 large handful fresh **flat leaf parsley**, roughly chopped

1 **red snapper**, about 450g/1lb, cleaned, with head and tail removed

1 **red** or **grey mullet**, about 500g/1¼lb, cleaned, with head and tail removed

350–450g/12oz–1lb thick **cod fillet**

400g/14oz can chopped **Italian plum tomatoes**

175g/6oz/1½ cups dried **fregola**

salt and freshly ground **black pepper** for seasoning

vermicelli with clam sauce

THIS **RECIPE** ORIGINATES FROM THE CALABRIAN CITY OF **NAPLES**, WHERE BOTH **FRESH TOMATO** SAUCE AND **LOCAL SEAFOOD** ARE TRADITIONALLY SERVED WITH **VERMICELLI**. HERE THE TWO ARE **COMBINED** TO MAKE A VERY **TASTY DISH**.

method

SERVES 4

1 Scrub the clams thoroughly under cold running water and discard any that are open or that do not close when sharply tapped against the work surface.

2 Pour the wine into a large saucepan, add the garlic cloves and half the parsley, then the clams. Cover tightly and bring to the boil over a high heat. Cook, shaking the pan frequently, for about 5 minutes, until the clams have opened.

3 Tip the clams into a large colander set over a bowl and let the liquid drain through. Leave the clams until cool enough to handle, then remove about two-thirds of them from their shells, tipping the clam liquor into the bowl of cooking liquid. Discard any clams that have not opened. Set both shelled and unshelled clams aside, keeping the unshelled clams warm in a bowl covered with a lid.

4 Heat the oil in a saucepan, add the onion and cook gently, stirring frequently, for about 5 minutes, until softened and lightly coloured. Add the tomatoes, then strain in the clam cooking liquid. Add the chilli and salt and pepper to taste. Bring to the boil, half cover the pan and simmer gently for 15–20 minutes.

5 Meanwhile, cook the pasta in lightly salted boiling water for about 8–10 minutes, until tender but still firm to the bite. Finely chop the remaining parsley.

6 Add the shelled clams to the tomato sauce, stir well and heat through very gently for 2–3 minutes.

7 Drain the cooked pasta well and tip it onto a warmed plate. Taste the sauce for seasoning, then pour the sauce over the pasta and toss well. Garnish with the reserved clams, sprinkle with parsley and serve.

ingredients

1kg/2¼lb fresh **clams**
250ml/8fl oz/1 cup **dry white wine**
2 **garlic** cloves, bruised
1 large handful fresh **flat leaf parsley**, roughly chopped, plus extra to garnish
30ml/2 tbsp **olive oil**
1 small **onion**, finely chopped
8 ripe **plum tomatoes**, peeled, seeded and finely chopped
½–1 fresh **red chilli**, seeded and finely chopped
350g/12oz dried **vermicelli**
salt and freshly ground **black pepper**

variations

When fresh clams are not in season, use two 200g/7oz jars clams in natural juice. Drain and rinse well before heating in the tomato sauce. Spaghetti or spaghettini can be used instead of vermicelli.

ingredients

300g/11oz/2 cups **broccoli florets**

40g/1½oz/½ cup **pine nuts**

350g/12oz/3 cups dried **orecchiette**

60ml/4 tbsp **olive oil**

1 small **red onion**, thinly sliced

50g/2oz jar **anchovies** in olive oil

1 **garlic** clove, crushed

50g/2oz/⅔ cup freshly grated **Pecorino cheese**

salt and freshly ground **black pepper**

orecchiette
with anchovies & broccoli

WITH ITS **ROBUST FLAVOURS**, THIS PASTA DISH IS VERY TYPICAL OF **SOUTHERN ITALIAN** AND **SICILIAN** COOKING. **ANCHOVIES**, PINE NUTS, **GARLIC** AND **PECORINO** CHEESE ARE ALL VERY POPULAR INGREDIENTS. SERVE WITH **CRUSTY ITALIAN BREAD** FOR A LIGHT LUNCH OR **SUPPER**.

method

SERVES 4

1 Break the broccoli florets into small sprigs and cut off the stalks. If the stalks are large, chop or slice them. Cook the broccoli florets and stalks in a saucepan of boiling salted water for 2 minutes, then drain and refresh under cold running water. Leave to drain on kitchen paper.

2 Put the pine nuts in a dry non-stick frying pan and toss over a low heat for 1–2 minutes, or until lightly toasted and golden. Remove and set aside.

3 Cook the pasta in lightly salted boiling water for 8–10 minutes, until tender but still firm to the bite.

4 Meanwhile, heat the oil in a frying pan, add the onion and fry gently, stirring frequently, for about 5 minutes, until softened. Add the anchovies with their oil, then add the garlic and fry over a medium heat, stirring frequently, for 1–2 minutes, until the anchovies break down to form a paste. Add the broccoli and plenty of pepper and toss over the heat for 1–2 minutes. Taste for seasoning.

5 Drain the pasta and tip it into a warmed bowl. Add the broccoli mixture and grated Pecorino and toss well to combine. Sprinkle the pine nuts over the top and serve immediately.

meat & poultry

tagliatelle with meat sauce

THIS RECIPE IS AN **AUTHENTIC** MEAT SAUCE – **RAGU** – FROM THE **CITY** OF **BOLOGNA** IN EMILIA-ROMAGNA. THE SAUCE IS VERY **RICH** AND IS **ALWAYS SERVED** WITH **TAGLIATELLE**, NEVER WITH SPAGHETTI.

method

SERVES 6–8

1 Make the meat sauce. Heat the butter and oil in a large frying pan or saucepan until sizzling. Add the chopped vegetables, garlic and the pancetta or bacon and cook over a medium heat, stirring frequently, for about 10 minutes, or until the vegetables have softened.

2 Add the minced beef and pork, lower the heat and cook gently for 10 minutes, stirring frequently and breaking up any lumps in the meat with a wooden spoon. Stir in salt and pepper to taste, then add the wine and stir again. Simmer for about 5 minutes, or until reduced.

3 Add the canned tomatoes and 250ml/8fl oz/1 cup of the beef stock and bring to the boil. Stir the sauce well, then lower the heat. Half cover the pan with a lid and leave to simmer very gently for 2 hours. Stir occasionally during this time and add more stock as it becomes absorbed.

4 Pour the cream into the sauce, stir well to mix, then simmer, without a lid, for a further 30 minutes, stirring frequently. Meanwhile, cook the pasta in lightly salted boiling water for 2–3 minutes, if fresh, or 8–10 minutes, if dried, until tender but still firm to the bite. Taste the sauce to check the seasoning. Drain the cooked pasta and tip it into a warmed bowl. Pour the sauce over the pasta and toss well. Serve immediately, sprinkled with grated Parmesan.

ingredients

450g/1lb fresh or
   dried **tagliatelle**
salt and freshly ground
   black pepper
freshly grated **Parmesan**
   cheese, to serve

For the Bolognese sauce
25g/1oz/2 tbsp **butter**
15ml/1 tbsp **olive oil**
1 **onion**, finely chopped
2 **carrots**, finely chopped
2 **celery** sticks, finely chopped
2 **garlic** cloves, finely chopped
130g/4½oz **pancetta** or
   rindless **streaky**
   bacon, diced
250g/9oz lean **minced beef**
250g/9oz lean **minced pork**
120ml/4fl oz/½ cup **dry**
   white wine
2 x 400g/14oz cans chopped
   plum tomatoes
475–750ml/16fl oz–1¼
   pints/2–3 cups **beef stock**
100ml/3½fl oz/scant ½ cup
   panna da cucina or
   double cream

ingredients

50g/2oz/ 4 tbsp **butter**

1 small **onion**, finely chopped

200g/7oz/1¾ cups **frozen peas**

100ml/3½fl oz/scant ½ cup
chicken stock

2.5ml/½ tsp **sugar**

175ml/6fl oz/¾ cup **dry
white wine**

350g/12oz fresh **fettuccine**

75g/3oz piece **cooked ham**,
cut into bite-size chunks

115g/4oz/1⅓ cups freshly grated
Parmesan cheese

salt and freshly ground
black pepper

fettuccine
with ham & peas

THIS **SIMPLE** DISH MAKES A VERY **GOOD**
FIRST COURSE FOR **SIX** PEOPLE OR A **MAIN**
COURSE FOR **THREE** TO FOUR. THE
INGREDIENTS ARE ALL EASILY **AVAILABLE**
FROM THE **SUPERMARKET** SO THE RECIPE
MAKES AN **IDEAL IMPROMPTU** SUPPER.

method

SERVES 3–6

1　Melt the butter in a medium frying pan or saucepan, add the onion
and cook over a low heat for about 5 minutes, until softened, but not
coloured. Add the peas, stock and sugar, with salt and pepper to taste.

2　Bring to the boil, then lower the heat and simmer for 3–5 minutes, or
until the peas are tender. Add the wine, increase the heat and boil until
the wine has reduced.

3　Cook the pasta in lightly salted boiling water for 2–3 minutes, until
tender but still firm to the bite. When it is almost ready, add the ham
to the sauce, with about a third of the grated Parmesan. Heat through,
stirring, then taste for seasoning.

4　Drain the pasta and tip it into a warmed serving bowl. Pour the sauce
over the pasta and toss well. Serve immediately, sprinkled with the
remaining grated Parmesan.

lasagne from bologna

THIS IS THE **CLASSIC** LASAGNE **AL FORNO**. IT IS **BASED** ON A RICH, **MEATY FILLING** – JUST AS YOU WOULD EXPECT FROM AN AUTHENTIC **BOLOGNESE** RECIPE.

method

SERVES 6

1 Preheat the oven to 190°C/375°F/Gas 5. If the Bolognese sauce is cold, reheat it. Once it is hot, stir in enough hot beef stock to make it quite runny.

2 Make the white sauce. Melt the butter in a medium saucepan, add the flour and cook, stirring, for 1–2 minutes. Add the milk, a little at a time, whisking vigorously after each addition. Bring to the boil and cook, stirring, until the sauce is smooth and thick. Add salt and pepper to taste, whisk well to mix, then remove from the heat.

3 Spread about a third of the Bolognese sauce over the base of an ovenproof dish.

4 Cover the Bolognese sauce in the base of the dish with about a quarter of the white sauce, followed by four sheets of lasagne. Repeat the layers twice more, then cover the top layer of lasagne with the remaining white sauce and sprinkle the grated Parmesan evenly over the top.

5 Bake for 40–45 minutes, or until the pasta feels tender when pierced with a skewer. Allow to stand for about 10 minutes before serving.

ingredients

1 quantity **Bolognese sauce** (see page 58)

150–250ml/5–8fl oz/⅔–1 cup hot **beef stock**

12 "no-need-to-pre-cook" **dried lasagne sheets**

50g/2oz/⅔ cup freshly grated **Parmesan cheese**

For the white sauce

50g/2oz/4 tbsp **butter**

50g/2oz/½ cup **plain flour**

900ml/1½ pints/3¾ cups hot **milk**

salt and freshly ground **black pepper**

cook's tips

The Bolognese sauce can be made up to 3 days in advance and kept in a covered container in the fridge. The lasagne is best baked straight after layering or the pasta will begin to absorb the sauces and dry out. To reheat leftover lasagne, prick it all over with a skewer, then slowly pour a little milk over to moisten. Cover with foil and reheat in a 190°C/375°F/Gas 5 oven for 20 minutes, or until bubbling.

ingredients

60ml/4 tbsp **olive oil**

250g/9oz boneless **lamb** neck
 fillet, diced quite small

2 **garlic** cloves, finely chopped

2 **bay leaves**, torn

250ml/8fl oz/1 cup **dry
 white wine**

4 ripe **plum tomatoes**, peeled
 and chopped

2 large **red peppers**, seeded
 and diced

salt and freshly ground
 black pepper

cook's tips

The peppers do not have to be red.
Use yellow, orange or green if
you prefer; either one colour or a
mixture. If you need to add water
to the sauce towards the end of
cooking, take it from the pan
used for cooking the pasta.
You can make your own fresh
maccheroni alla chitarra or buy
the dried pasta from an Italian
delicatessen. Alternatively, this
sauce is just as good with ordinary
long or short macaroni. You will
need 350–425g/12–15oz.

lamb & sweet pepper sauce

THIS SIMPLE SAUCE IS A **SPECIALITY** OF
THE **ABRUZZO-MOLISE** REGION, EAST OF
ROME, WHERE IT IS TRADITIONALLY SERVED
WITH **MACCHERONI ALLA CHITARRA** —
SQUARE-SHAPED LONG **MACARONI**.

method

SERVES 4–6

1 Heat half the olive oil in a medium frying pan or saucepan, add the
   pieces of lamb and sprinkle with a little salt and pepper. Cook the
   meat over a medium to high heat, stirring frequently, for about
   10 minutes, until it is browned on all sides.

2 Sprinkle in the garlic and add the bay leaves, then pour in the wine
   and let it bubble until reduced.

3 Add the remaining oil, the tomatoes and the peppers and stir to mix.
   Season again. Cover with the lid and simmer over a low heat for
   45–55 minutes, or until the lamb is very tender. Stir occasionally
   during cooking and moisten with water if the sauce becomes too dry.
   Remove the bay leaves from the sauce before serving it with pasta.

ingredients

400g/14oz spicy
  pork sausages
30ml/2 tbsp **olive oil**
1 small **onion**, finely chopped
2 **garlic** cloves, crushed
1 large **yellow pepper**, seeded
  and cut into strips
5ml/1 tsp **paprika**
5ml/1 tsp dried **mixed herbs**
5–10ml/1–2 tsp **chilli sauce**
400g/14oz can **plum tomatoes**
250–300ml/8–10fl oz/1–1¼
  cups **vegetable stock**
300g/11oz/2¾ cups fresh or
  dried **fusilli**
salt and freshly ground
  black pepper
freshly grated **Pecorino cheese**,
  to serve

fusilli with sausage

SPICY HOT **SAUSAGE** AND **TOMATO** SAUCE COMBINE WITH **SPIRALS** OF PASTA TO MAKE THIS REALLY **TASTY** DISH FROM **SOUTHERN ITALY**. PECORINO CHEESE, WITH ITS **STRONG** AND **SALTY** FLAVOUR, IS THE PERFECT **ACCOMPANIMENT**. SERVE IT AT AN INFORMAL SUPPER PARTY WITH A **FULL-BODIED RED WINE** AND LOTS OF CRUSTY ITALIAN **COUNTRY BREAD.**

method

SERVES 4

1 Grill the sausages for 10–12 minutes, until they are browned on all sides, then drain them on kitchen paper.

2 Heat the oil in a large frying pan or saucepan, add the onion and garlic and cook over a low heat, stirring frequently, for 5–7 minutes, until soft. Add the yellow pepper, paprika, herbs and chilli sauce to taste. Cook gently, stirring occasionally, for 5–7 minutes.

3 Tip in the canned tomatoes, breaking them up with a wooden spoon, then add salt and pepper to taste and stir well. Cook over a medium heat for 10–12 minutes, adding the vegetable stock gradually as the sauce reduces.

4 While the tomato sauce is cooking, cut the grilled sausages diagonally into 1cm/½in pieces. Add the sausage pieces to the sauce, reduce the heat to low and cook for 10 minutes.

5 Meanwhile, cook the pasta in lightly salted boiling water for about 2–3 minutes, if fresh, or 8–10 minutes, if dried, until tender but still firm to the bite.

6 Taste the sauce for seasoning. Drain the pasta, add it to the pan of sauce, toss well, then divide among four warmed bowls. Sprinkle with a little Pecorino and serve, with more Pecorino handed separately.

bucatini with sausage & pancetta

THIS IS A VERY **RICH** AND **SATISFYING** MAIN COURSE DISH. IT **HARDLY** NEEDS **GRATED PARMESAN** CHEESE AS AN ACCOMPANIMENT, BUT YOU CAN **HAND** SOME ROUND IN A **SEPARATE** BOWL IF YOU WISH.

method

SERVES 4

1 Remove any skin from the sausagemeat and break the meat up roughly with a knife. Process the tomatoes in a food processor or blender to a purée.

2 Heat the oil in a medium frying pan or saucepan, add the garlic and fry over a low heat for 1–2 minutes. Remove the garlic with a slotted spoon and discard it.

3 Add the pancetta or bacon and the sausagemeat and cook over a medium heat for 3–4 minutes. Stir constantly with a wooden spoon to break up the sausagemeat – it will become brown and look crumbly.

4 Add the puréed tomatoes to the pan with half the parsley and salt and pepper to taste. Stir well and bring to the boil, scraping up any sediment from the sausagemeat that has stuck to the base of the pan.

5 Lower the heat, cover and simmer, stirring occasionally, for 30 minutes. Taste the sausagemeat sauce for seasoning.

6 Meanwhile, cook the pasta in lightly salted boiling water for 8–10 minutes, until tender but still firm to the bite.

7 Put the cream and egg yolks in a warmed large bowl and mix with a fork. As soon as the pasta is tender, drain it well and add it to the bowl of cream mixture. Toss until the pasta is coated, then pour the sausagemeat sauce over the pasta and toss again. Serve immediately, sprinkled with the remaining parsley.

ingredients

115g/4oz **pork sausagemeat**
400g/14oz can **plum tomatoes**
15ml/1 tbsp **olive oil**
1 **garlic** clove, crushed
115g/4oz **pancetta** or
    rindless **streaky bacon**,
    roughly chopped
30ml/2 tbsp chopped fresh **flat**
    leaf parsley
400g/14oz dried **bucatini**
60–75ml/4–5 tbsp **panna da**
    cucina or **double cream**
2 **egg yolks**
salt and freshly ground
    black pepper

cook's tips

To save time processing the tomatoes, use passata.
For authenticity, buy salsiccia a metro, a pure pork sausage sold by the metre at Italian delicatessens.
Bucatini is a long hollow pasta that looks like hard drinking straws; spaghetti works equally well.

pappardelle with rabbit sauce

THIS **RICH-TASTING** DISH COMES FROM **NORTHERN ITALY**, WHERE **RABBIT** SAUCES FOR **PASTA** ARE VERY **POPULAR**. PAPPARDELLE ARE ATTRACTIVE BROAD **RIBBON NOODLES** WITH **WAVY** EDGES AND ARE GOOD WITH MEAT AND **GAME** DISHES. DRIED PAPPARDELLE IS BECOMING POPULAR.

method

SERVES 4

1 Put the dried mushrooms in a bowl, pour over the warm water and leave to soak for 15–20 minutes. Heat the butter and oil in a frying pan or saucepan until just sizzling. Add the chopped vegetables, pancetta or bacon and the parsley and cook for about 5 minutes.

2 Add the pieces of rabbit and fry on both sides for 3–4 minutes. Pour the wine over and let it reduce for a few minutes, then add the tomatoes or passata. Drain the mushrooms and pour the soaking liquid into the pan.

3 Chop the mushrooms and add them to the mixture, with the bay leaves and salt and pepper to taste. Stir well, cover and simmer, stirring occasionally, for 35–40 minutes, until the rabbit is tender.

4 Remove the pan from the heat and lift out the pieces of rabbit with a slotted spoon. Cut them into bite-size chunks and stir them into the sauce. Remove and discard the bay leaves. Taste the sauce and add more salt and pepper, if needed.

5 Cook the pasta in lightly salted boiling water for 2–3 minutes, if fresh, or 8–10 minutes, if dried, until tender but still firm to the bite.

6 Meanwhile, reheat the sauce. Drain the pasta and transfer it to a warmed serving bowl. Add the sauce and toss thoroughly to combine. Serve immediately, sprinkled with parsley.

ingredients

15g/½oz dried **porcini mushrooms**
175ml/6fl oz/¾ cup warm **water**
25g/1oz/2 tbsp **butter**
15ml/1 tbsp **olive oil**
1 small **onion**, finely chopped
½ **carrot**, finely chopped
½ **celery** stick, finely chopped
40g/1½oz **pancetta** or rindless **streaky bacon**, chopped
15ml/1 tbsp roughly chopped fresh **flat leaf parsley**, plus extra to garnish
250g/9oz boneless **rabbit** meat
90ml/6 tbsp **dry white wine**
200g/7oz can chopped **Italian plum tomatoes** or 200ml/ 7fl oz/scant 1 cup **passata**
2 **bay leaves**, partly torn
300g/11oz fresh or dried **pappardelle**
salt and freshly ground **black pepper**

ingredients

60ml/4 tbsp **olive oil**

1 **onion**, finely chopped

1 **carrot**, finely chopped

2 **garlic** cloves, crushed

2 ripe **plum tomatoes**, peeled
    and finely chopped

130g/4½oz **minced beef**

130g/4½oz **minced pork**

250g/9oz **minced chicken**

30ml/2 tbsp **brandy**

25g/1oz/2 tbsp **butter**

90ml/6 tbsp **panna da cucina**
    or **double cream**

16 dried **cannelloni tubes**

75g/3oz/1 cup freshly grated
    Parmesan cheese

salt and freshly ground
    black pepper

green salad, to serve

For the white sauce

50g/2oz/4 tbsp **butter**

50g/2oz/½ cup **plain flour**

900ml/1½ pints/3¾ cups **milk**

nutmeg

mixed meat cannelloni

A **CREAMY**, RICH **FILLING** AND SAUCE MAKE THIS AN **UNUSUAL** CANNELLONI.

method

SERVES 4

1 Heat the oil in a medium frying pan, add the onion, carrot, garlic and tomatoes and cook over a low heat, stirring, for about 10 minutes, or until very soft.

2 Add all the minced meats to the pan and cook gently for about 10 minutes, stirring frequently to break up any lumps. Add the brandy, increase the heat and stir until it has reduced, then add the butter and cream and cook gently, stirring occasionally, for about 10 minutes. Allow to cool.

3 Preheat the oven to 190°C/375°F/Gas 5. Make the white sauce. Melt the butter in a medium saucepan, add the flour and cook, stirring, for 1–2 minutes. Add the milk, a little at a time, whisking vigorously after each addition. Bring to the boil and cook, stirring, until the sauce is smooth and thick. Grate in fresh nutmeg to taste, then season with salt and pepper and whisk well. Remove the pan from the heat.

4 Spoon a little of the white sauce into a baking dish. Fill the cannelloni tubes with the meat mixture and place in a single layer in the dish. Pour the remaining white sauce over them, then sprinkle with the Parmesan. Bake for 35–40 minutes, or until the pasta feels tender when pierced with a skewer. Allow to stand for 10 minutes before serving with a green salad.

---

cook's tip
Instead of using dried cannelloni tubes you could roll fresh lasagne sheets around the meat filling.

---

ingredients

350g/12oz **minced beef**

1 **egg**

60ml/4 tbsp roughly chopped fresh **flat leaf parsley**

2.5ml/½ tsp crushed **dried red chillies**

1 thick slice **white bread**, crusts removed

30ml/2 tbsp **milk**

about 30ml/2 tbsp **olive oil**

300ml/½ pint/1¼ cups **passata**

400ml/14fl oz/1¾ cups **vegetable stock**

5ml/1 tsp **sugar**

350–450g/12oz–1lb fresh or dried **spaghetti**

salt and freshly ground **black pepper**

freshly grated **Parmesan cheese**, to serve

spaghetti with meatballs

TINY MEATBALLS SIMMERED IN A **SWEET** AND **SPICY** TOMATO SAUCE ARE **TRULY DELICIOUS** WITH SPAGHETTI. **CHILDREN LOVE** THEM, AND YOU CAN **EASILY** LEAVE OUT THE **CHILLIES**.

method

SERVES 6–8

1 Put the minced beef in a large bowl. Add the egg, and half the parsley and crushed chillies. Season with plenty of salt and pepper.

2 Tear the bread into small pieces and place in a small bowl. Moisten with the milk. Leave to soak for a few minutes, then squeeze out the excess milk and crumble the bread over the meat mixture. Mix everything together with a wooden spoon, then use your hands to squeeze and knead the mixture until it is smooth and quite sticky.

3 Rinse your hands in cold water, then pick up small pieces of the mixture and roll them between your palms to make about 60 very small balls. Place the meatballs on a tray and chill in the fridge for about 30 minutes.

4 Heat the oil in a large, deep non-stick frying pan. Cook the meatballs, in batches, until browned on all sides. Pour the passata and stock into the pan. Heat gently, then add the remaining chillies and the sugar, with salt and pepper to taste. Return all the meatballs to the pan. Bring to the boil, lower the heat and cover. Simmer for 20 minutes.

5 Cook the pasta in lightly salted boiling water for 2–3 minutes, if fresh, or for 8–10 minutes, if dried, until tender but still firm to the bite. Drain and tip it into a warmed large bowl. Pour the sauce over the pasta and toss gently. Sprinkle with the remaining parsley and serve with grated Parmesan handed separately.

conchiglie
with chicken livers & herbs

FRESH HERBS AND **CHICKEN LIVERS** ARE A GOOD COMBINATION, OFTEN USED TOGETHER ON **CROSTINI** IN **TUSCANY**. HERE THEY ARE **TOSSED** WITH **PASTA SHELLS** TO MAKE A VERY TASTY **SUPPER DISH**.

method

SERVES 4

1 Melt half the butter in a medium frying pan or saucepan, add the pancetta or bacon and fry over a medium heat for a few minutes until it is lightly coloured but not crisp.

2 Add the chicken livers, garlic, half the sage and plenty of pepper. Increase the heat and cook the livers, stirring frequently, for about 5 minutes, until they change colour all over.

3 Cook the pasta in lightly salted boiling water for 8–10 minutes, until tender but still firm to the bite.

4 Meanwhile, pour the wine over the chicken livers in the pan and let it sizzle, then lower the heat and simmer gently for 5 minutes.

5 Add the remaining butter to the pan. As soon as it has melted, add the diced tomatoes, toss to mix, then add the remaining sage and the parsley. Stir well. Taste and add salt if needed.

6 Drain the pasta and tip it into a warmed bowl. Pour the sauce over and toss well. Serve immediately.

ingredients

50g/2oz/4 tbsp **butter**
115g/4oz **pancetta** or rindless
 streaky bacon, diced
250g/9oz frozen **chicken livers**,
 thawed, drained and diced
2 **garlic** cloves, crushed
10ml/2 tsp chopped fresh **sage**
300g/11oz/2¾ cups dried
 conchiglie
150ml/¼ pint/⅔ cup **dry**
 white wine
4 ripe **plum tomatoes**, peeled
 and diced
15ml/1 tbsp chopped fresh **flat**
 leaf parsley
salt and freshly ground
 black pepper

penne with chicken, broccoli & cheese

THE COMBINATION OF **BROCCOLI**, GARLIC AND **GORGONZOLA** IS VERY GOOD, AND GOES **ESPECIALLY WELL** WITH **CHICKEN**.

method

SERVES 4

1 Plunge the broccoli into a saucepan of boiling salted water. Bring back to the boil and boil for 2 minutes, then drain in a colander and refresh under cold running water. Shake well to remove the surplus water and set aside to drain completely.

2 Melt the butter in a large frying pan or saucepan, add the chicken and garlic, with salt and pepper to taste, and stir well. Fry over a medium heat for 3 minutes, or until the chicken becomes white.

3 Cook the pasta in lightly salted boiling water for 8–10 minutes, until tender but still firm to the bite.

4 Pour the wine and cream over the chicken mixture in the pan, stir to mix, then simmer, stirring occasionally, for about 5 minutes, until the sauce has reduced and thickened. Add the broccoli, increase the heat and toss to mix it with the chicken. Taste for seasoning.

5 Drain the pasta and tip it into the sauce. Add the Gorgonzola and toss well. Serve with grated Parmesan.

ingredients

115g/4oz/scant 1 cup **broccoli florets**, divided into tiny sprigs
50g/2oz/4 tbsp **butter**
2 skinless **chicken** breast fillets, cut into thin strips
2 **garlic** cloves, crushed
400g/14oz/3½ cups dried **penne**
120ml/4fl oz/½ cup **dry white wine**
200ml/7fl oz/scant 1 cup **panna da cucina** or **double cream**
90g/3½oz **Gorgonzola cheese**, rind removed and diced small
salt and freshly ground **black pepper**
freshly grated **Parmesan cheese**, to serve.

variation
Use leeks instead of broccoli if you prefer. Fry them with the chicken.

ingredients

15g/½oz dried **porcini mushrooms**

175ml/6fl oz/¾ cup warm **water**

25g/1oz/2 tbsp **butter**

1 small **leek** or 4 **spring onions**, chopped

1 **garlic** clove, crushed

1 small handful fresh **flat leaf parsley**, roughly chopped

120ml/4fl oz/½ cup **dry white wine**

250ml/8fl oz/1 cup **chicken stock**

400g/14oz fresh or dried **pappardelle**

2 skinless **chicken** breast fillets, cut into thin strips

105ml/7 tbsp **mascarpone cheese**

salt and freshly ground **black pepper**

fresh **basil leaves**, shredded, to garnish

pappardelle
with chicken & mushrooms

RICH AND **CREAMY**, THIS DISH IS ONE OF EVERYONE'S **FAVOURITES**.

method

SERVES 4

1 Put the dried mushrooms in a bowl. Pour in the warm water and leave to soak for about 15–20 minutes. Tip into a fine sieve set over a bowl and squeeze the mushrooms with your hands to release as much liquid as possible. Chop the mushrooms finely and set aside the strained soaking liquid until required.

2 Melt the butter in a medium frying pan or saucepan, add the chopped mushrooms, leek or spring onions, garlic and parsley, with salt and pepper to taste.

3 Cook over a low heat, stirring frequently, for about 5 minutes, then pour in the wine and stock and bring to the boil. Lower the heat and simmer for about 5 minutes, or until the liquid has reduced and is thickened.

4 Meanwhile, cook the pasta in lightly salted boiling water, adding the reserved soaking liquid from the mushrooms to the water, for 2–3 minutes, if fresh, or 8–10 minutes, if dried, until tender but still firm to the bite.

5 Meanwhile, add the chicken strips to the sauce and simmer for 5 minutes, or until just tender. Add the mascarpone, a spoonful at a time, stirring well after each addition, then add one or two spoonfuls of the water used for cooking the pasta. Taste for seasoning.

6 Drain the pasta and tip it into a warmed large bowl. Add the chicken and sauce and toss well. Serve immediately, topped with the shredded basil leaves.

variations

Add 115g/4oz/1 cup sliced button or chestnut mushrooms with the chicken. Add blanched sprigs of broccoli before the mascarpone in step 5.

vegetarian

penne with artichokes

ARTICHOKES ARE A VERY **POPULAR** VEGETABLE IN **ITALY**, AND ARE OFTEN USED IN **SAUCES** FOR PASTA. THIS SAUCE IS **GARLICKY** AND **RICHLY** FLAVOURED, THE PERFECT **DINNER PARTY** FIRST COURSE DURING THE **GLOBE ARTICHOKE SEASON**.

method

SERVES 6

1 Have ready a bowl of cold water mixed with the lemon juice. Cut off the artichoke stalks, then discard the outer leaves until only the pale inner leaves remain. Cut off their tops. Cut the base in half lengthways, then prise out the hairy choke. Cut the artichokes lengthways into 5mm/¼in slices, adding them to the bowl of acidulated water.

2 Bring a pan of salted water to the boil. Drain the artichokes, add them immediately to the water and boil for 5 minutes, drain and set aside.

3 Heat the oil in a large frying pan and cook the fennel, onion, parsley and garlic over a medium heat, stirring frequently, for 10 minutes. Add the tomatoes and wine, with salt and pepper to taste. Bring to the boil, stirring, lower the heat, cover and simmer for 10–15 minutes. Stir in the artichokes, cover and simmer for 10 minutes more.

4 Meanwhile, cook the pasta in lightly salted boiling water for 8–10 minutes, until tender but still firm to the bite.

5 Drain the pasta. Stir the capers into the sauce, then taste for seasoning. Tip the pasta into a warmed bowl, pour the sauce over and toss well. Serve immediately, garnished with the fennel fronds. Hand the Parmesan separately.

ingredients

juice of ½ **lemon**

2 **globe artichokes**

30ml/2 tbsp **olive oil**

1 small **fennel bulb**, thinly sliced, with feathery tops reserved

1 **onion**, finely chopped

1 handful fresh **flat leaf parsley**, roughly chopped

4 **garlic** cloves, finely chopped

400g/14oz can chopped **plum tomatoes**

150ml/¼ pint/⅔ cup **dry white wine**

350g/12oz/3 cups dried **penne**

10ml/2 tsp **capers**, chopped

salt and freshly ground **black pepper**

freshly grated **Parmesan cheese**, to serve

ingredients

1 **red pepper**, seeded and cut
   into 1cm/½in squares
1 **yellow** or **orange pepper**,
   seeded and cut into
   1cm/½in squares
1 small **aubergine**, roughly diced
2 **courgettes**, roughly diced
75ml/5 tbsp extra virgin **olive oil**
15ml/1 tbsp chopped fresh **flat
   leaf parsley**
5ml/1 tsp dried **oregano**
250g/9oz baby **plum tomatoes**,
   hulled and halved lengthways
2 **garlic** cloves, roughly chopped
350–400g/12–14oz/3–3½ cups
   dried **conchiglie**
salt and freshly ground
   black pepper
4–6 fresh **marjoram** or
   oregano sprigs, to garnish

cook's tip
Pasta and roasted vegetables are
good served cold, so if you have
any of this dish left over, cover it
tightly with clear film, chill in the
fridge overnight and serve it the
next day as a salad.
It would also make a particularly
good salad to take on a picnic.

conchiglie with roasted vegetables

NOTHING COULD BE **SIMPLER** – OR MORE
DELICIOUS – THAN TOSSING FRESHLY
COOKED **PASTA** WITH **ROASTED
VEGETABLES**. THE FLAVOUR IS **SUPERB**.

method

SERVES 4–6

1 Preheat the oven to 190°C/375°F/Gas 5. Rinse the prepared peppers,
   aubergine and courgettes in a sieve or colander under cold running
   water, drain, then tip the vegetables into a large roasting tin.

2 Pour 45ml/3 tbsp of the olive oil over the vegetables and sprinkle with
   the fresh and dried herbs. Add salt and pepper to taste and stir well.
   Roast for about 30 minutes, stirring two or three times.

3 Stir the halved tomatoes and chopped garlic into the vegetable
   mixture, then roast for 20 minutes more, stirring once or twice.

4 Meanwhile, cook the pasta in lightly salted boiling water for about
   8–10 minutes, until tender but still firm to the bite.

5 Drain the pasta and tip it into a warmed bowl. Add the roasted
   vegetables and the remaining oil and toss well. Serve the pasta and
   vegetables in warmed bowls, garnished with herb sprigs.

rigatoni with wild mushrooms

THIS IS A GOOD **SAUCE** TO MAKE FROM **STORE CUPBOARD INGREDIENTS** BECAUSE IT DOESN'T RELY ON ANYTHING FRESH, APART FROM THE **FRESH HERBS**.

method

SERVES 4–6

1 Put the dried mushrooms in a bowl, pour the warm water over and soak for 15–20 minutes. Tip into a fine sieve set over a bowl and squeeze the mushrooms to release as much liquid as possible. Reserve the mushrooms and the strained liquid.

2 Heat the oil in a medium frying pan and fry the shallots, garlic and herbs over a low heat, stirring frequently, for about 5 minutes. Add the mushrooms and butter and stir until the butter has melted. Season well. Stir in the tomatoes and the reserved liquid from the soaked mushrooms. Bring to the boil, then cover, lower the heat and simmer, stirring occasionally, for about 20 minutes.

3 Meanwhile, cook the pasta in lightly salted boiling water for about 8–10 minutes, until tender but still firm to the bite.

4 Taste the sauce for seasoning. Drain the pasta, reserving some of the cooking water, and tip it into a large warmed bowl. Add the sauce and the grated Parmesan and toss to mix. Add a little cooking water if you prefer a runnier sauce. Serve immediately, garnished with marjoram and with more Parmesan handed around separately.

> ### variation
> For a richer sauce, add a few spoonfuls of panna da cucina, cream or mascarpone to the sauce just before serving.

ingredients

2 x 15g/½oz packets dried
porcini mushrooms
175ml/6fl oz/¾ cup
warm **water**
30ml/2 tbsp **olive oil**
2 **shallots**, finely chopped
2 **garlic** cloves, crushed
a few fresh **marjoram sprigs**,
leaves stripped and finely
chopped, plus extra to garnish
1 handful fresh **flat leaf**
parsley, chopped
25g/1oz/2 tbsp **butter**, diced
400g/14oz can chopped
plum tomatoes
400g/14oz/3½ cups dried
rigatoni
25g/1oz/⅓ cup freshly grated
Parmesan cheese, plus extra
to serve
salt and freshly ground
black pepper

THIS IS THE **PESTO** FOR REAL **ROCKET LOVERS**. THE TASTE IS **SHARP** AND **PEPPERY**, AND DELICIOUS FOR A **SUMMER PASTA** MEAL WITH A GLASS OF **CHILLED DRY WHITE** WINE.

ingredients

4 **garlic** cloves

90ml/6 tbsp **pine nuts**

2 large handfuls **rocket**, about 150g/5oz, stalks removed

50g/2oz/⅔ cup freshly grated **Parmesan cheese**

50g/2oz/⅔ cup freshly grated **Pecorino cheese**

90ml/6 tbsp extra virgin **olive oil**

400g/14oz fresh or dried **spaghetti**

salt and freshly ground **black pepper**

freshly grated **Parmesan** and **Pecorino cheese**, to serve

spaghetti with rocket pesto

method

SERVES 4

1 Put the garlic and pine nuts in a blender or food processor and process until finely chopped.

2 Add the rocket, Parmesan and Pecorino, olive oil and salt and pepper to taste and process for 5 seconds. Stop and scrape down the side of the bowl. Process for a further 5–10 seconds, until a smooth paste is formed.

3 Cook the spaghetti in lightly salted boiling water for 2–3 minutes, if fresh, or 8–10 minutes, if dried, until tender but still firm to the bite.

4 Turn the pesto into a large bowl. Just before the pasta is ready, add 1–2 ladlefuls of the cooking water to the pesto and stir well to mix.

5 Drain the pasta, tip it into the bowl of pesto and toss well to mix. Serve immediately, with the grated cheeses handed separately.

variation

To temper the flavour of the rocket and make the pesto milder, add 115g/4oz/½ cup ricotta or mascarpone cheese to the pesto in step 4 and mix well before adding the water.

ingredients

50g/2oz/4 tbsp **butter**

30ml/2 tbsp extra virgin **olive oil**

1 small **onion**, thinly sliced

200g/7oz small **courgettes**,
   cut into thin julienne strips

1 **garlic** clove, crushed

10ml/2 tsp finely chopped
   fresh **marjoram**

350g/12oz/3 cups
   dried **strozzapreti**

1 large handful **courgette**
   flowers, thoroughly washed
   and dried

salt and freshly ground
   black pepper

thin shavings of **Parmesan**
   cheese, to serve

cook's tip

Strozzapreti or "priest stranglers"
are a special kind of short pasta
shape from Modena. You can buy
packets of them in Italian
delicatessens, or use gemelli, a
similar kind of twisted pasta.

strozzapreti with courgette flowers

THIS **PRETTY**, SUMMERY DISH IS **STREWN**
WITH **COURGETTE FLOWERS** BUT YOU
CAN MAKE IT EVEN IF YOU DON'T HAVE
THE FLOWERS. IN ITALY, **BUNCHES** OF
COURGETTE FLOWERS ARE A COMMON
SIGHT ON **VEGETABLE STALLS** DURING
THE SUMMER, AND ARE **FREQUENTLY**
USED FOR **STUFFING** AND COOKING.

method

SERVES 4

1 Heat the butter and half the olive oil in a medium frying pan or
   saucepan, add the sliced onion and cook gently, stirring frequently,
   for about 5 minutes, until softened. Add the courgettes to the pan
   and sprinkle with the crushed garlic, chopped marjoram and salt and
   pepper to taste. Cook for 5–8 minutes, until the courgettes have
   softened, but are not coloured, turning them over from time to time.

2 Meanwhile, cook the pasta in lightly salted boiling water for about
   8–10 minutes, until tender but still firm to the bite.

3 Set aside a few whole courgette flowers for the garnish, then roughly
   shred the rest and add them to the courgette mixture. Stir to mix and
   taste for seasoning.

4 Drain the pasta, tip it into a large warmed bowl and add the remaining
   oil. Toss, add the courgette mixture and toss again. Top with the
   Parmesan shavings and serve immediately.

three-colour tagliatelle

method

COURGETTES AND **CARROTS** ARE CUT INTO **DELICATE RIBBONS** SO THAT WHEN THEY ARE **COOKED** AND **TOSSED** WITH TAGLIATELLE THEY **LOOK LIKE COLOURED PASTA**. SERVE AS A **SIDE DISH** OR SPRINKLE WITH FRESHLY GRATED PARMESAN CHEESE FOR A **LIGHT STARTER** OR **VEGETARIAN MAIN COURSE**.

1 With a vegetable peeler, cut the courgettes and carrots into long thin ribbons. Bring a large pan of salted water to the boil, then add the courgette and carrot ribbons. Bring the water back to the boil and boil for 30 seconds, then drain and set aside.

2 Cook the pasta in lightly salted water for 2–3 minutes, until tender but still firm to the bite.

3 Drain the pasta and return it to the pan. Add the vegetable ribbons, oil, garlic and salt and pepper and toss over a medium heat until the mixture is glistening with oil. Serve with extra roasted garlic, if liked.

ingredients

2 large **courgettes**

2 large **carrots**

250g/9oz fresh **egg tagliatelle**

60ml/4 tbsp extra virgin **olive oil**

flesh of 2 roasted **garlic** cloves, plus extra roasted **garlic** cloves, to serve (optional)

salt and freshly ground **black pepper**

cook's tip

To roast garlic, put a whole head of garlic on a lightly oiled baking sheet. Place in a preheated oven at 180°C/350°F/Gas 4 and roast for about 30 minutes. Remove the garlic from the oven and set aside. When cool enough to handle, dig out the flesh from the cloves with the point of a knife. If you don't want to go to the trouble of roasting garlic, you can use crushed raw garlic, but the flavour will be stronger.

tagliatelle with broccoli & spinach

THIS IS AN **EXCELLENT VEGETARIAN SUPPER** DISH. IT IS **NUTRITIOUS AND FILLING** AND NEEDS NO ACCOMPANIMENT. IF YOU LIKE, YOU CAN USE **TAGLIATELLE** FLECKED WITH **HERBS**.

method

SERVES 4

1 Put the broccoli in the basket of a steamer, cover and steam over boiling water for 10 minutes. Add the spinach, cover and steam for 4–5 minutes, or until both are tender. Towards the end of the cooking time, sprinkle the vegetables with freshly grated nutmeg and salt and pepper to taste. Transfer the vegetables to a colander.

2 Add salt to the water in the steamer and fill the steamer pan with boiling water, then add the pasta and cook 2–3 minutes, if fresh, or 8–10 minutes, if dried, until tender but still firm to the bite. Meanwhile, chop the broccoli and spinach in the colander.

3 Drain the pasta. Heat 45ml/3tbsp oil in the pasta pan, add the pasta and chopped vegetables and toss over a medium heat until evenly mixed. Sprinkle in the lemon juice and plenty of black pepper, then taste and add more lemon juice, oil, salt and nutmeg if you like. Serve immediately, sprinkled liberally with freshly grated Parmesan and black pepper.

ingredients

2 heads of **broccoli**
450g/1lb fresh **spinach**,
   stalks removed
nutmeg
450g/1lb fresh or dried **egg
   tagliatelle**
about 45ml/3 tbsp extra virgin
   olive oil
juice of half a **lemon**, or to taste
salt and freshly ground **black
   pepper**
freshly grated **Parmesan
   cheese**, to serve

variations

If you like, add a sprinkling of crushed dried chillies with the black pepper in step 3.
To add both texture and protein, garnish the finished dish with one or two handfuls of toasted pine nuts. They are often served with broccoli and spinach in Italy.

ingredients

45ml/3 tbsp **pine nuts**

350g/12oz dried **paglia e fieno**

45ml/3 tbsp extra virgin **olive oil**

30ml/2 tbsp **sun-dried
tomato paste**

2 pieces drained **sun-dried
tomatoes** in olive oil, cut into
very thin slivers

40g/1½oz **radicchio leaves**,
finely shredded

4–6 **spring onions**, thinly sliced
into rings

salt and freshly ground
black pepper

cook's tip

If you find the presentation too
fiddly, you can toss the sun-dried
tomato and radicchio mixture with
the pasta in one large warmed
bowl before serving, then serve it
sprinkled with the spring onions
and toasted pine nuts.

paglia e fieno with sun-dried tomatoes

THIS IS A **LIGHT**, **MODERN** PASTA DISH
OF THE KIND SERVED IN **FASHIONABLE
RESTAURANTS**. IT IS THE **PRESENTATION**
THAT SETS IT APART, NOT THE PREPARATION,
WHICH IS VERY **QUICK** AND **EASY**.

method

SERVES 4

1 Put the pine nuts in a non-stick frying pan and toss over a low to
medium heat for 1–2 minutes, or until they are lightly toasted and
golden. Remove and set aside.

2 Cook the pasta in lightly salted boiling water for 8–10 minutes,
keeping the colours separate by using two pans.

3 While the pasta is cooking, heat 15ml/1 tbsp of the oil in a medium
skillet or saucepan. Add the sun-dried tomato paste and the sun-dried
tomatoes, then stir in 2 ladlefuls of the water used for cooking the
pasta. Simmer until the sauce is slightly reduced, stirring constantly.

4 Mix in the shredded radicchio, then taste and season if necessary.
Keep on a low heat. Drain the paglia e fieno, keeping the colours
separate, and return them to the pans in which they were cooked.
Add about 15ml/1 tbsp oil to each pan and toss over a medium to
high heat until the pasta is glistening with the oil.

5 Arrange a portion of green and white pasta in each of four warmed
bowls, then spoon the sun-dried tomato and radicchio mixture in the
centre. Sprinkle the spring onions and toasted pine nuts decoratively
over the top and serve immediately. Before eating, each diner should
toss the sauce ingredients with the pasta to mix well.

ingredients

400g/14oz fresh or
   dried **spaghetti**
90ml/6 tbsp extra virgin **olive oil**
2–4 **garlic** cloves, crushed
1 dried **red chilli**
1 small handful fresh **flat
   leaf parsley**,
   roughly chopped
salt

cook's tips

Since the oil is such an important
ingredient here, use only the very
best cold-pressed extra virgin
olive oil.
Don't use salt in the oil
and garlic mixture, because it will
not dissolve sufficiently. This is why
plenty of salt is recommended for
cooking the pasta.
In Rome, grated Parmesan is
never served with this dish, nor
is it seasoned with pepper.
In summer, Romans use fresh
chillies, which they grow in pots on
their terraces and window ledges.

spaghetti with garlic & oil

IN **ROME** THEY RUN THE WORDS TOGETHER
TO PRONOUNCE THE NAME OF THIS DISH,
SPAGHETTI **AGLIO E OLIO**, AS "**SPAGHETTI-
AYO-E-OYO**". SOMETIMES IT IS GIVEN
ITS FULL NAME OF **SPAGHETTI AGLIO,
OLIO E PEPERONCINO** BECAUSE **CHILLI –
PEPERONCINO** – IS ALWAYS INCLUDED
TO GIVE THE DISH **SOME BITE**.

method

SERVES 4

1 Cook the pasta in well-salted boiling water for 2–3 minutes, if fresh,
or 8–10 minutes, if dried, until tender but still firm to the bite.

2 Meanwhile, heat the oil very gently in a small frying pan or saucepan.
Add the garlic and dried chilli and stir over a low heat until the garlic
is just beginning to brown.

3 Drain the pasta and tip it into a large, warmed bowl. Pour on the oil
and garlic mixture, add the parsley and toss vigorously until the pasta
glistens. Serve immediately.

orecchiette with rocket

THIS **HEARTY DISH** IS FROM **PUGLIA** IN THE SOUTH-EAST OF ITALY. SERVE IT AS A MAIN COURSE WITH **COUNTRY BREAD**. SOME **DELICATESSENS** AND SUPER-MARKETS SELL A FARMHOUSE-STYLE **ITALIAN LOAF** CALLED **PUGLIESE**, WHICH WOULD BE EXTREMELY **APPROPRIATE**.

method

SERVES 4–6

1 Heat 15ml/1 tbsp of the olive oil in a medium saucepan, add half the finely chopped onion and cook gently, stirring frequently, for about 5 minutes, until softened. Add the canned tomatoes or passata, oregano and chilli powder or cayenne pepper to the onion. Pour the wine over, if using, and add a little salt and pepper to taste. Cover the pan and simmer, stirring occasionally, for about 15 minutes.

2 Bring a large saucepan of salted water to the boil. Add the potatoes and pasta. Stir well and let the water return to the boil. Lower the heat and simmer for 15 minutes, or according to the instructions on the packet, until the pasta is cooked.

3 Heat the remaining oil in a large frying pan or saucepan, add the remaining onion and the garlic and fry, stirring occasionally, for 2–3 minutes. Add the rocket, toss over the heat for about 2 minutes, until wilted, then stir in the tomato sauce and the ricotta. Mix well.

4 Drain the pasta and potatoes, add both to the pan of sauce and toss to mix. Taste for seasoning and serve immediately in warmed bowls, with grated Pecorino handed separately.

cook's tip
Orecchiette are always slightly chewy. When making this dish, it is traditional to cook them in the same pan as the potatoes, but if you are unsure of getting the timing right, cook them separately.

ingredients

45ml/3 tbsp **olive oil**
1 small **onion**, finely chopped
300g/11oz canned chopped
plum tomatoes or **passata**
2.5ml/½ tsp dried **oregano**
pinch of **chilli powder** or
    cayenne pepper
about 30ml/2 tbsp **red** or **white**
    wine (optional)
2 **potatoes**, about 200g/
    7oz, diced
300g/11oz/2¾ cups
    dried **orecchiette**
2 **garlic** cloves, finely chopped
150g/5oz **rocket leaves**, stalks
    removed, shredded
90g/3½oz/scant ½ cup
    ricotta cheese
salt and freshly ground
    black pepper
freshly grated **Pecorino cheese,**
    to serve

eliche with pesto

BOTTLED **PESTO** IS A **USEFUL STAND-BY**, BUT IF YOU HAVE A FOOD PROCESSOR, IT IS **VERY EASY** TO **MAKE YOUR OWN**.

ingredients

50g/2oz/1⅓ cups fresh
   basil leaves, plus fresh
   basil sprigs, to garnish
2–4 **garlic** cloves
60ml/4 tbsp **pine nuts**
120ml/4fl oz/½ cup extra virgin
   olive oil
115g/4oz/1⅓ cups freshly grated
   Parmesan cheese, plus
   extra to serve
25g/1oz/⅓ cup freshly grated
   Pecorino cheese
400g/14oz/3½ cups dried **eliche**
salt and freshly ground
   black pepper

method

SERVES 4

1 Put the basil leaves, garlic and pine nuts in a blender or food processor. Add 60ml/4 tbsp of the olive oil. Process until the ingredients are finely chopped, then stop the machine, remove the lid and scrape down the sides of the bowl.

2 Turn the machine on again and slowly pour the remaining oil in a thin, steady stream through the feeder tube. You may need to stop the machine and scrape down the sides of the bowl once or twice to make sure everything is evenly mixed.

3 Scrape the mixture into a large bowl and beat in the cheeses with a wooden spoon. Taste and add salt and pepper if necessary.

4 Cook the pasta in lightly salted boiling water for 8–10 minutes, until tender but still firm to the bite. Drain well, then add it to the bowl of pesto and toss well. Serve immediately, garnished with the fresh basil sprigs. Serve grated Parmesan separately.

---

cook's tip
Pesto can be made up to 2–3 days in advance. To store pesto, transfer it to a small bowl and pour a thin film of olive oil over the surface. Cover the bowl tightly with clear film and keep it in the fridge.

pasta with mushrooms

SERVED WITH **WARMED CIABATTA**, THIS **SIMPLE** DISH MAKES AN **EXCELLENT** CHOICE FOR A **VEGETARIAN** SUPPER.

method

SERVES 4

1 Put the dried porcini mushrooms in a bowl with the warm water and leave to soak for 15–20 minutes. Tip into a sieve set over a bowl and squeeze the porcini with your hands to release as much liquid as possible. Reserve the strained soaking liquid. Chop the porcini finely.

2 Heat the oil and cook the garlic, parsley, sun-dried tomato strips and porcini over a low heat, stirring frequently, for about 5 minutes. Stir in the wine, simmer for a few minutes until reduced, then stir in the chestnut mushrooms. Pour in the stock and simmer, uncovered, for 15–20 minutes more, until the liquid has reduced and is quite thick.

3 Cook the pasta in lightly salted water for 8–10 minutes, until tender but still firm to the bite.

4 Taste the mushroom sauce for seasoning. Drain the pasta, reserving a little of the cooking liquid, and tip it into a warmed large bowl. Add the sauce and toss, thinning it if necessary with a little cooking water. Serve immediately, sprinkled with rocket and/or chopped parsley.

> ### variation
> Fresh wild mushrooms can be used instead of chestnut mushrooms, but they are seasonal and often expensive. A cheaper alternative is to use a box of mixed wild mushrooms. These are sold in many supermarkets.

ingredients

15g/½oz dried **porcini mushrooms**

175ml/6fl oz/¾ cup warm **water**

45ml/3 tbsp **olive oil**

2 **garlic** cloves, finely chopped

1 handful fresh **flat leaf parsley**, roughly chopped

2 large pieces drained **sun-dried tomato** in olive oil, sliced into thin strips

120ml/4fl oz/½ cup **dry white wine**

225g/8oz/2 cups **chestnut mushrooms**, thinly sliced

475ml/16fl oz/2 cups **vegetable stock**

450g/1lb/4 cups dried short **pasta shapes**, such as ruote, penne, fusilli or eliche

salt and freshly ground **black pepper**

rocket and/or fresh **flat leaf parsley**, to garnish

ingredients

400g/14oz/3½ cups
  dried **elicoidale**
3 **egg yolks**
105ml/7 tbsp freshly grated
  Parmesan cheese
200g/7oz/scant 1 cup
  ricotta cheese
60ml/4 tbsp **panna da cucina**
  or **double cream**
nutmeg
40g/1½oz/3 tbsp **butter**
salt and freshly ground
  black pepper

cook's tip
Elicoidale are a short tubular pasta with curved ridges. If you can't get them, use rigatoni, which have straight ridges.

elicoidale with cheese & cream

ALTHOUGH THE **INGREDIENTS** FOR THIS DISH ARE QUITE PLAIN, THE **COMBINATION** IS VERY **APPETIZING**. IT IS VERY **QUICK**, AND ALL YOU NEED IS A TUB OF **RICOTTA** IN THE FRIDGE FOR A **SWIFT** AND **SIMPLE EVENING MEAL**.

method

SERVES 4

1 Cook the pasta in lightly salted boiling water for 8–10 minutes, until tender but still firm to the bite.

2 Meanwhile, mix the egg yolks, grated Parmesan and ricotta together in a bowl. Add the cream and mix with a fork.

3 Grate in nutmeg to taste, then season with plenty of black pepper and a little salt. Drain the pasta thoroughly when cooked. Return the clean pan to the heat. Melt the butter, add the drained pasta and toss vigorously over a medium heat.

4 Turn off the heat under the pan and add the ricotta mixture. Stir well with a large spoon for 10–15 seconds, until all the pasta is coated in sauce. Serve immediately in warmed individual bowls.

salads

pasta salade niçoise

ALONG THE **MEDITERRANEAN** COAST, WHERE **ITALY** MEETS **FRANCE**, THE **CUISINES** OF BOTH COUNTRIES HAVE MANY **SIMILARITIES**. IN THIS SALAD THE INGREDIENTS OF A **CLASSIC FRENCH** SALADE NIÇOISE ARE GIVEN A MODERN **ITALIAN TWIST**.

method

SERVES 4

1 Cook the beans in a large pan of salted boiling water for 5–6 minutes. Remove the beans with a large slotted spoon and refresh under cold running water.

2 Add the pasta to the same pan of cooking water, bring back to the boil and cook for 8–10 minutes, until tender but still firm to the bite.

3 Meanwhile, heat a ridged cast-iron pan over a low heat. Dip a wad of kitchen paper in the oil, wipe it over the surface of the pan and heat gently. Brush the tuna steaks on both sides with oil and sprinkle liberally with pepper. Add to the pan and cook over a medium to high heat for 1–2 minutes on each side. Remove and set aside.

4 Drain the cooked pasta well and tip into a large bowl. Add the remaining oil, the beans, tomato quarters, black olives, anchovies, parsley, lemon juice and salt and pepper to taste. Toss well to mix, then leave to cool.

5 Flake or slice the tuna into large pieces, discarding the skin, then fold it into the salad. Taste the salad for seasoning. Arrange the chicory leaves on the inside of a large shallow bowl. Spoon the pasta salad into the centre and serve with lemon wedges.

> ### cook's tip
> Don't overcook the tuna or it will be dry. Fresh tuna is always best slightly pink or rare in the centre. If you prefer, you can use canned tuna. Drain and flake a 175g/6oz can tuna in olive oil and fold it gently into the pasta in step 5. You can also use cos or Little Gem lettuce leaves instead of chicory.

ingredients

115g/4oz **French beans**, cut into 5cm/2in lengths
250g/9oz/2¼ cups dried **penne rigate**
105ml/7 tbsp extra virgin **olive oil**
2 fresh **tuna steaks**, total weight 350–450g/12oz–1lb
6 baby **plum tomatoes**, quartered lengthways
50g/2oz/½ cup pitted black **olives**, halved lengthways
6 bottled or canned **anchovies** in olive oil, drained and chopped
30–45ml/2–3 tbsp chopped fresh **flat leaf parsley**, to taste
juice of ½–1 **lemon**
2 heads of **chicory**, leaves separated
salt and freshly ground **black pepper**
lemon wedges, to serve

ingredients

225g/8oz/2 cups dried
   chifferini or **pipe rigate**
450g/1lb ripe baby **plum**
   tomatoes, halved lengthways
75ml/5 tbsp extra virgin **olive oil**
2 **garlic** cloves, cut into
   thin slivers
30ml/2 tbsp **balsamic vinegar**
2 pieces **sun-dried tomato** in
   olive oil, drained and chopped
pinch of **sugar**
1 handful **rocket**, about
   65g/2½oz
salt and freshly ground
   black pepper

variation
If you are in a hurry and don't have time to roast the tomatoes, you can make the salad with halved raw tomatoes instead. If you like, add 150g/5oz mozzarella cheese, drained and diced, with the rocket in step 4.

roasted cherry tomato & rocket salad

THIS IS A GREAT **SIDE SALAD** TO ACCOMPANY **BARBECUED** CHICKEN, STEAKS OR CHOPS. ROASTED TOMATOES ARE **VERY JUICY**, WITH AN **INTENSE**, **SMOKY-SWEET** FLAVOUR.

method

SERVES 4

1 Preheat the oven to 190°C/375°F/ Gas 5. Cook the pasta in salted boiling water for 8–10 minutes, until tender but still firm to the bite.

2 Arrange the halved tomatoes, cut-side up, in a roasting tin, drizzle 30ml/2 tbsp of the oil over them and sprinkle with the slivers of garlic and salt and pepper to taste. Roast in the oven for 20 minutes, turning once.

3 Put the remaining oil in a large bowl with the vinegar, sun-dried tomato, sugar and a little salt and pepper to taste. Stir well to mix. Drain the pasta, add it to the bowl of dressing and toss to mix. Add the roasted tomatoes and mix gently.

4 Before serving, add the chopped rocket, toss lightly and taste for seasoning. Serve either at room temperature or chilled.

chargrilled pepper salad

THIS IS A GOOD SIDE SALAD TO SERVE WITH **PLAIN GRILLED** OR **BARBECUED** CHICKEN OR **FISH**. THE INGREDIENTS ARE **SIMPLE** AND **FEW**, BUT THE OVERALL **FLAVOUR** IS WONDERFULLY **INTENSE**.

method

SERVES 4

1 Put the peppers under a hot grill for about 10 minutes, turning them frequently until they are charred on all sides. Put the hot peppers in a plastic bag, seal the bag and set aside until they are cool.

ingredients

2 large **peppers** (red and green)
250g/9oz/2¼ cups dried
　fusilli tricolore
1 handful fresh **basil leaves**
1 handful fresh
　coriander leaves
1 **garlic** clove
salt and freshly ground
　black pepper

For the dressing
30ml/2 tbsp bottled **pesto**
juice of ½ **lemon**
60ml/4 tbsp extra virgin **olive oil**

---
cook's tip
Serve the salad at room temperature or chilled, whichever you prefer.
---

2 Meanwhile, cook the pasta in lightly salted boiling water for 8–10 minutes, until tender but still firm to the bite.

3 Whisk all the dressing ingredients together in a large bowl. Drain the cooked pasta well and tip it into the bowl of dressing. Toss well to mix and set aside to cool.

4 Remove the peppers from the bag and hold them one at a time under cold running water. Peel off the charred skins with your fingers, split the peppers open and pull out the cores. Rub off all the seeds under the running water, then pat the peppers dry on kitchen paper.

5 Chop the peppers and add them to the pasta. Put the basil, coriander and garlic on a board and chop them all together. Add to the pasta and toss to mix, then taste for seasoning and serve, garnished with a few whole basil and coriander leaves.

ingredients

450g/1lb fresh **mussels**

250ml/8fl oz/1 cup **dry**
  white wine

2 **garlic** cloves, roughly chopped

1 handful fresh
  flat leaf parsley

175g/6oz/1 cup prepared
  squid rings

175g/6oz/1½ cups small dried
  pasta shapes

175g/6oz/1 cup peeled
  cooked **prawns**

For the dressing

90ml/6 tbsp extra virgin **olive oil**

juice of 1 **lemon**

5–10ml/1–2 tsp **capers**,
  roughly chopped

1 **garlic** clove, crushed

1 small handful fresh
  flat leaf parsley,
  finely chopped

salt and freshly ground
  black pepper

seafood salad

THIS IS A VERY **SPECIAL SALAD** WHICH CAN BE SERVED AS A **FIRST COURSE** OR **MAIN MEAL**. THE CHOICE OF **PASTA SHAPE** IS UP TO YOU, BUT ONE OF THE UNUSUAL **"DESIGNER" SHAPES** WOULD SUIT IT WELL.

method

SERVES 4–6

1 Scrub the mussels under cold running water. Discard any that are damaged or open or that do not close when sharply tapped against the work surface.

2 Pour half the wine into a large saucepan, add the garlic, parsley and mussels. Cover the pan tightly and bring to the boil over a high heat. Cook, shaking the pan frequently, for about 5 minutes, until the mussels have opened.

3 Tip the mussels into a colander set over a bowl and let the cooking liquid drain through. Leave the mussels until cool enough to handle, then remove them from their shells, tipping the liquid from the mussels into the bowl of cooking liquid. Discard any mussels that are closed.

4 Return the mussel cooking liquid to the pan and add the remaining wine and the squid rings. Bring to the boil, cover and simmer gently, stirring occasionally, for 30 minutes, or until the squid is tender. Leave the squid to cool in the cooking liquid.

5 Meanwhile, cook the pasta in lightly salted water for 8–10 minutes, until tender but still firm to the bite and whisk all the dressing ingredients in a large bowl, adding a little salt and pepper to taste. Drain well, add to the bowl of dressing and mix. Leave to cool.

6 Tip the cooled squid into a sieve and drain well, then rinse it lightly under cold running water. Add the squid, mussels and prawns to the dressed pasta and toss thoroughly to mix. Cover the bowl tightly with clear film and chill in the fridge for about 4 hours. Toss well and adjust the seasoning to taste before serving.

ingredients

175g/6oz **broccoli** florets,
   divided into small sprigs
225g/8oz/2 cups dried **farfalle**
2 large cooked **chicken breasts**

For the dressing
90g/3½oz **Gorgonzola cheese**
15ml/1 tbsp **white**
   wine vinegar
60ml/4 tbsp extra virgin **olive oil**
2.5–5ml/½–1tsp finely chopped
   fresh **sage**, plus extra **sage**
   sprigs to garnish
salt and freshly ground
   black pepper

chicken &
broccoli salad

GORGONZOLA MAKES A **TANGY** DRESSING
THAT GOES WELL WITH BOTH **CHICKEN** AND
BROCCOLI. SERVE FOR A **LUNCH** OR **SUPPER**
DISH, WITH CRUSTY **ITALIAN** BREAD.

method
SERVES 4

1 Cook the broccoli florets in a large saucepan of salted boiling water
for 3 minutes. Remove with a slotted spoon and rinse under cold
running water, then spread out on kitchen paper to drain and dry.

2 Add the pasta to the broccoli cooking water, then bring back to the
boil and cook for 8–10 minutes, until tender but still firm to the bite.
Drain in a colander, rinse under cold running water until cold, then
leave to drain and dry, shaking the colander occasionally.

3 Remove the skin from the cooked chicken breasts and cut the meat
into bite-size pieces.

4 Make the dressing. Put the cheese in a large bowl and mash with a
fork, then whisk in the wine vinegar, followed by the oil and sage and
salt and pepper to taste.

5 Add the pasta, chicken and broccoli. Toss well, then season to taste
and serve, garnished with sage.

pasta salad with salami & olives

method

THE **GARLIC** AND **HERB DRESSING** GIVES A **MEDITERRANEAN** FLAVOUR TO A HANDFUL OF INGREDIENTS FROM THE **STORE CUPBOARD** AND **FRIDGE**, MAKING THIS AN EXCELLENT SALAD FOR **WINTER**. THERE ARE MANY **DIFFERENT** TYPES OF ITALIAN **SALAMI** THAT CAN BE USED. **SALAME NAPOLETANO** IS COARSE CUT AND **PEPPERY**, WHILE **SALAME MILANESE** IS FINE CUT AND **MILD** IN FLAVOUR.

1 Cook the pasta in lightly salted water for 8–10 minutes, until tender but still firm to the bite.

2 Meanwhile, make the dressing. Put all the ingredients for the dressing in a large bowl with a little salt and pepper to taste, and whisk thoroughly to mix.

3 Drain the pasta well, add it to the bowl of dressing and toss to mix. Leave the dressed pasta to cool, stirring occasionally.

4 When the pasta is cold, add the remaining ingredients and toss well to mix again. Taste for seasoning, then serve immediately, garnished with basil leaves.

ingredients

225g/8oz/2 cups dried **gnocchi** or **conchiglie**

50g/2oz/½ cup pitted **black olives**, quartered lengthways

75g/3oz thinly sliced **salami**, skin removed, diced

½ small **red onion**, finely chopped

1 large handful fresh **basil leaves**, shredded, plus extra whole leaves to serve

For the dressing

60ml/4 tbsp extra virgin **olive oil**

pinch of **sugar**

juice of ½ **lemon**

5ml/1 tsp **Dijon mustard**

10ml/2 tsp dried **oregano**

1 **garlic** clove, crushed

salt and freshly ground **black pepper**

tuna & sweetcorn salad

THIS IS AN EXCELLENT **MAIN COURSE** SALAD FOR A **SUMMER LUNCH** OUTSIDE. IT **TRAVELS** VERY WELL, SO IT IS GOOD FOR **PICNICS**, TOO.

ingredients

175g/6oz/1½ cups dried **conchiglie**

175g/6oz can **tuna** in olive oil, drained and flaked

175g/6oz can **sweetcorn**, drained

75g/3oz **bottled roasted red peppers**, rinsed, dried and finely chopped

1 handful fresh **basil leaves**, chopped, plus a few extra whole leaves to serve

salt and freshly ground **black pepper**

For the dressing
60ml/4 tbsp extra virgin **olive oil**
15ml/1 tbsp **balsamic vinegar**
5ml/1 tsp **red wine vinegar**
5ml/1 tsp **Dijon mustard**
5–10ml/1–2 tsp **honey**

method

SERVES 4

1 Cook the pasta in lightly salted water for 8–10 minutes, until tender but still firm to the bite. Drain in a colander and rinse under cold running water. Leave until cold, shaking the colander occasionally.

2 Make the dressing. Put the oil in a large bowl, add the two kinds of vinegar and whisk well together until emulsified. Add the mustard, honey and salt and pepper to taste and whisk again until thick.

3 Add the pasta to the dressing and toss well to mix, then add the tuna, sweetcorn and roasted pepper and toss again. Mix in about half the basil and taste for seasoning. Serve at room temperature or chilled, with the remaining basil sprinkled on top.

> ### variation
> To save time, you could use canned sweetcorn with peppers.

---

pink & green salad

SPIKED WITH A LITTLE **FRESH CHILLI**, THIS PRETTY SALAD MAKES A **DELICIOUS LIGHT LUNCH** SERVED WITH **HOT CIABATTA** ROLLS AND A BOTTLE OF **SPARKLING** DRY ITALIAN **WHITE WINE**. PRAWNS AND AVOCADO MAKE A **WINNING COMBINATION**, SO IT'S ALSO A GOOD CHOICE FOR A **BUFFET PARTY**.

ingredients

225g/8oz/2 cups dried **farfalle**

juice of ½ **lemon**

1 small fresh **red chilli**, seeded and very finely chopped

60ml/4 tbsp chopped fresh **basil**

30ml/2 tbsp chopped fresh **coriander**

60ml/4 tbsp extra virgin **olive oil**
15ml/1 tbsp **mayonnaise**
250g/9oz/1½ cups peeled cooked **prawns**
1 **avocado**
salt and freshly ground **black pepper**

method

SERVES 4

1 Cook the pasta in lightly salted boiling water for 8–10 minutes, until tender but still firm to the bite.

2 Meanwhile, put the lemon juice and chilli in a bowl with half the basil and coriander and salt and pepper to taste. Whisk well to mix, then whisk in the oil and mayonnaise until thick. Add the prawns and gently stir to coat in the dressing.

3 Drain the pasta in a colander, and rinse under cold running water until cold. Leave to drain and dry, shaking the colander occasionally.

4 Halve, stone and peel the avocado, then cut the flesh into neat diced pieces. Add to the prawns and dressing with the pasta, toss well to mix and taste for seasoning. Serve immediately, sprinkled with the remaining basil and coriander.

> ### cook's tip
> This pasta salad can be made hours ahead of time, without the avocado. Cover the bowl with clear film and chill in the fridge. Prepare the avocado and add it to the salad just before serving or it will discolour.